ELIZABETH HILLIARD AND STAFFORD CLIFF

PAINT

THE FIRED EARTH BOOK
OF NATURAL COLOUR

PAVILION

PAINT

First published in Great Britain in 2001 by
PAVILION BOOKS LIMITED
London House, Great Eastern Wharf
Parkgate Road, London SW11 4NQ
www.pavilionbooks.co.uk

Designed by Stafford Cliff
Production Artwork by Ian Hammond
Picture Research by Nadine Bazar

Quotation on pp156–157 from
Reminiscences, (1913) by Kandinsky

A CIP catalogue record for this book is
available from the British Library.

ISBN 1 86205 368 5

Set in Frutiger and Tekton
Repro at Alliance Graphics, Singapore and
    Bedford
Printed at Imago, Singapore

2 4 6 8 10 9 7 5 3 1

This book can be ordered direct from the
publisher. Please contact the Marketing
Department. But try your bookshop first.

'Colour, or lack c
our lives in almc
aspect, and the
choose in terms
or the interiors
make statement
the lifestyles th

f it, informs

st every

colours we

of our clothes,

of our houses,

s about us and

at we lead.' Kelly Hoppen

forget

paint

think

colour

now think of some more

old newspapers, crusty bread, shoe polish, a new penny, nutmeg, nasturtiums, hollyberry, green cherry, faded denim, celery, conker, flying jacket, butter, gumboots, blackboard, full moon, mackintosh, cornflower, banana, carrot, tennis ball, tomato, egg yolk, milk, red cabbage, lettuce, terracotta pot, chocolate sauce, smooth pebbles, bright lipstick, white chalk, ocean, sand dunes, hanging ivy, thick mud, coffee, strawberry jam, moss, cinnamon sticks, sugar cubes, rosebuds, cranberries, peeling bark, lambs' wool, red wine, orange peel, ice cubes, jelly beans, daisy chain.

Foreword *by Kevin McCloud* Of all the precious minerals, beautiful landscapes, sights, experiences and astonishing materials the world has to offer, it amazes me that paint can still exercise a power of wonder over the human mind. Perhaps it is because paint is a vehicle for colour, a conduit for chromatic concupiscence. More probably it's because paint has the power to cleanse, renew and change our visual world: our walls and homes, cars and furniture, our faces and nails.

And paint has always been powerful. Socially, it used to be more influential than it is now. For tens of thousands of years it has been used to mark territory, cover faces and decorate the otherwise humdrum paraphernalia of our lives.

The great red Berber city of Taroudant on the edges of the Moroccan Sahara is that colour because of the iron oxide in its clay walls and paint, and yet today it still makes an awesome statement about community and power.

Indoors, the power of paint is no less exciting. The early cave paintings of bison and men at Lascaux that were executed in soot, red earth and glue mixed together, are early attempts at human expression through art, as eight thousand years ago the citizens of Jericho were also painting rooms using colour. Similarly, the Romans developed the fine art of mural painting and *trompe l'oeil* perspective in exotic paints pigmented with fine and strongly coloured minerals from the far corners of the Empire.

A limited and simple palette based on mineral pigments, and to a large extent on cheap powdered clays, formed the bulk of decorating colours right up until the middle of the twentieth century, basically enforcing a limited colour range that took on something of the quality of the natural world. The reason for this is obvious: those pigments, mainly iron oxides are also the colorants in the soil, rock, stone and sand around us.

By contrast, it's now possible to synthesize sixteen million separate colours (but mercifully not all are in production). Chemical technology has also multiplied in twenty years the types of paint you can buy. Whereas in the 1950s you could buy oil gloss, distemper or emulsion (standard formulations that even a painter in Jericho might recognize), there are now thousands of product types. These are the fruit born of new petro-chemistry, synthetic dye and pigment manufacture and also social changes such as health and eco awareness and changes in health and safety legislation.

All this choice may or may not be helpful. To the romantics among us, though, paint is as ever a vital part of our lives. It can camouflage or display, hide or assert. When worn and bruised it can tell the story of a place or object. It can be the vehicle for pattern or design. It can also, in the hands of an artist, be the stuff of dreams, creating a view into another world. This book celebrates what paint can do, and is a hymn to its versatility, a paean to its power.

Introduction Paint is today's and tomorrow's most versatile and effective decorating material. It is also one of the oldest mediums in existence for sealing and enlivening the structures that form our living spaces. To the best of our knowledge, paint has been used in every age and culture, across history and the world. *Paint: The Fired Earth Book of Natural Colour* approaches paint from a different perspective, through the power of colour with all its sensual possibilities. Taking its inspiration from images, tones and textures found in the wider world, this book offers a positive opportunity to explore the glorious variety of colour, through the medium of paint.

From the most basic mud concoctions discovered millennia past or the brilliance of the **mineral-based paints** of grand eighteenth-century houses in Europe and America, to the kaleidoscope of **chemical colours** and baffling range of finishes offered by manufacturers at the dawn of the twenty-first century, paint has been paramount. Like a latter-day Orlando, paint continues to reinvent itself, changing and adapting to the **modern age**.

Colour, meanwhile, is one of the luxuries of the modern world. Even a hundred years ago there simply were not the colours we take for granted today in decorating, homeware, clothing and everything else around us. Never before in history has such choice been available, and never so easily or inexpensively. Yet we rarely allow our eyes to dwell on the colour of things around us, for the sheer pleasure of looking, so that the **tones and hues** take on a life of their own. Looking at colour must be one of the cheapest forms of pleasure available. The only cost is time. Take the time to look at colour, to absorb it, before using it in your **home**.

This book asks you to think colour before paint. First, free yourself from the practicalities of **choosing and applying paint**, and think only, purely, of colour. Many of the pictures in this book are not of interiors at all, but instead explore the simple emotional power of colour. They open a window onto the vast landscape that is our **colour sourcebook**, a landscape full of surprises, subtle and sensuous.

Fired Earth is well known for its fine and **natural products** for the home – from terracotta tiles and Persian tribal rugs to solid hardwood flooring and so much else besides. Its paint colours take their inspiration from history, landscape and the natural world, and so do we in this book.

To help make sense of the riches of this world of colour, we have chosen six groupings or **families of tones** that have a natural alliance, each one represented by a particular terrain. Each chapter roams around its subject, looking at the natural world and at the human psychological associations with the colours in that group. It explores the ways that painted colour can be used to make our homes more beautiful, at the same time as taking an intelligent interest in the history and development of paint and pigment as a manufactured product.

Our first chapter, *Arctic Tints*, is devoted to variations of that exquisite concept, white, by which so many other colours are defined in the modern world. It celebrates the exquisite tones that we see around us in salt, chalk, cheese, flour and milk, in snow, frost and the froth on the sea's waves as they break on the shore. The importance of light in our surroundings and how this affects our use of colour is explored here.

Ocean Wash, the second chapter, celebrates the full range of blues summoned by mountains and distant hillsides, flowing water, the iridescence of a peacock's feather, the sea and hot azure sky. Here blues meld into mauves, verging towards purple.

Forest Hues revels in the landscape of fields and woodland, springy moss and lush leafy scenes, as well as delicious pea green and sparkling emerald. This chapter also considers yellower tones such as olive, mustard and egg yolk, as well as citrus lime green.

The countless shades of brown, deep red and russet form a natural family called *Earth Tones*. Think of soil, the rich darkness of mud, terracotta and peat. Allow yourself to be seduced by chocolate, ripe fruit, nuts, autumn leaves, the flames in a bonfire and its glowing embers.

Desert Shades looks at the soft neutrals, pale hues and shady greys that engage us with subtlety – colours that have gained a great following in recent decades. Draw inspiration for these tones from sand and stone, string and paper, slate and charcoal, pebbles and shells on the beach, and the tones of watercolour skies after rain.

The last chapter celebrates an explosion of colour. *Kaleidoscope* offers a joyful exploration of contemporary bright colours and the multicolour carnival you make when you throw them together. Shades of every colour belong to this family, jostling with each other for attention in a noisy, joyous mix of sunshine yellow, burnt orange, scarlet, turquoise and fluorescent orange, pink and green.

Fashions in colour come and go. But the contemporary aesthetic, more than any other before now, allows us to choose a mood or style that suits us, that is personal to us as individuals, rather than conforming to an imposed concept of acceptability. At the same time, in the modern world there is a marked overflow from one area of design into another. This often begins with the fashion industry: once a tone of lilac or lemon has been seen on the catwalk, it will soon appear in furnishing fabrics. When the fashion press dubs grey or brown 'the new black', it is not long before seductive shades of these colours are on sale in the form of irresistibly desirable cushions, china, fabric and...paint. Other forms of design are also influential. For example, shimmery metallic paint has been available on cars for years and now it is an accepted part of the home decorator's repertoire.

In this context, the popularity of paint as a decorating material is easy to understand. Inexpensive and widely available in a ravishing choice of colours and finishes, paint is easy to use, easy to change and produces startling transformations of interiors, quickly. So speedy is painting, in tune with the demands of contemporary culture, that within a day you can be inspired by a colour, go out to buy the paint that matches it, and (given the necessary practical conditions) have it on the wall, floor or ceiling. Or on the sill or skirting, or on a piece of furniture. Or, in fact, almost anywhere you care to mention...

There are plenty of do-it-yourself manuals to advise you how to apply paint. This book isn't one of them, although through it you will learn many useful and practical facts about paint and ways of using it. Instead, *Paint: The Fired Earth Book of Natural Colour* celebrates the decoration of our homes with painted colour, through passion, sensuality, emotion and inspiration.

ARC
TIN

CTICTS

White snow, white ice, white-out...white as far as the eye can see. What a relief, after the stress of a busy day, to think white. Cool, calm, serene white. Pure, innocent white. Dreamy, soothing, clean white, on which to float into a state of carefree bliss.

White rooms appeal to us because they feel pure and empty, with plenty of space for contemplation and meditation in a hectic world. Perhaps no other colour has more imagery associated with it. White is pure, white is virginal, white is shriven-clean. Think of hoar frost on foliage, drawing the shape of each leaf and twig with delicate outline. Picture soft cumulus clouds scudding across a windy sky, the crest of foaming waves breaking on the shore, or frothy bubbles in the bath. White doesn't only come in one uniform tone. Think of soap lather. Compare the white of the polar bear's fur or its teeth with the icy tundra on which it stands. There is milk white, yoghurt, curd cheese, poached-egg white, lily white, white roses, cow parsley, tulips and hyacinths. Imagine the papery skin of a garlic bulb, streaked with purple, the creamy flesh of a coconut.

White does not, of course, have a monopoly on powerful images and associations but, unlike some other colours, it suggests simplicity and honesty, an innocence and idealism to which we aspire in this chaotic modern world of ours.

There is another aspect to the colour white which makes it desirable in decorating terms. No other colour says 'modern' to us as loudly and clearly as white. No matter what style or period of home you live in, you can paint the walls and ceiling of a room white (and the floor too – why not?), add white blinds or shutters, install unfussy furniture or cover what is already there with white linen or cotton covers, crisp, loose and friendly. Instantly, you have the modern look.

The all-white approach can be an end in itself or it can be the starting point for a gradual build-up of other colours, subtle or powerful. It can be all-embracing, or it can provide a background for a few special pieces of furniture or art. In any circumstances and whatever its other qualities, an all-white interior is sharp and uncompromising.

Paint is the natural choice of material for bringing white into our homes. Snowy marble, fabric or carpet bring sensual texture, but the solid background of wall mass is usually provided by paint. No one, after all, would consider hanging plain white wallpaper (except as a lining for coloured or patterned wallpaper), even were such a thing available.

Not everyone agrees about white's beauty, of course. Some would say it isn't even a colour in its own right, some that it is cold, which indeed it can be if poorly lit. Some people use it to blot out existing horrors while waiting for inspiration about which 'real' colour to introduce. Others live white as a creed, surrounding themselves with furnishings and objects that trumpet a dedicated (and sometimes totally impractical) contemporaneity. Somewhere in between these extreme views comes a more pragmatic but nonetheless youthful attitude to white: as a cool, refreshing, light-enhancing and versatile surface finish. Use it alone, use it with colours of all families...white is pure joy.

There are certain ironies behind the ravishing simplicity of white. The main one is that there is in fact no definitive colour 'white'. White comes in countless shades, just like any other colour. Chalk White, Gypsum, Buxton White, Orchid, Tusk...these are just a few of the names given to white paint, each name trying to pinpoint the quality that defines this particular shade. Set against each other, some look creamy, some pinker, some bluer. The paint shade widely sold as 'brilliant' white is actually relatively blue. For a while in the 1980s (and such paints are still available), manufacturers promoted ready-mixed tinted whites, such as 'Rose White' and 'Apple White'.

The popularity and modernity of white are nothing new. White has its place in the palette of historic colours alongside a full range of rich and mellow tones. In the sixteenth century, the writer William Harrison expressed his preference for ceilings of 'delectable whitenesse'. Not long after, the poet Robert Herrick (1591–1674) wrote the memorable lines:

'Fain would I kiss my Julia's dainty leg,
Which is as white and hairless as an egg.'

Whites from a range of historic paint colours tend to be softer than brilliant white and they increase the decorator's choice, making white an even more versatile option. There is a white for every eventuality – one that will offer a soothing contrast to polished wooden floors, one to offset bathroom china and prevent the room looking clinical, another to provide a sympathetic background for the mellow colours of antique rugs or oil paintings hung on the walls, and another to support the lovely worn-out tones of vintage fabrics.

In contemporary decorating, white has two quite distinct assets – its relationship with light, both natural and artificial, and also with colour, be it bright or mellow.

Natural light from the sun is the source of all life on earth and is one of the most sought-after elements in decorating today – 'maximizing daylight' is a constant theme. White is the perfect colour for achieving this since it reflects more light than any other. The only danger is that white alone can be cold, especially if there is little natural light or the room faces north (in the northern hemisphere), which is where white's partnership with colour is so valuable. A white ceiling may seem a cliché, but it is very useful for reflecting light effectively. In certain circumstances, a coloured ceiling can work well with white on the walls, for example, in a room with an interestingly shaped or sloping ceiling, or where you want white walls to offset the colour of works of art or craft. White walls also create a spacious, cool backdrop for furniture that is interesting by merit of its form or colour, or both.

White is supposed to make a space feel bigger, but may simply make it feel chilly if you use it without other colours, even in small amounts, to lift and warm it. Used cleverly, in either the background or the foreground but probably not both, with areas or touches of red or brown or blue, for example, and with artificial lighting that is mellow and avoids glare, white can indeed be a space enhancer.

Planning your lighting scheme is a vital part of decorating a room. Artificial light is available in a huge choice of types (tungsten, halogen, fluorescent and so on), each with distinctive qualities which help them fulfil different functions. Lighting fitments are also available in a wide range of forms, from purely functional task lighting to kinetic light sculptures where the movement of light has a purely aesthetic purpose. Static light can be purely decorative too, either in the traditional form of lamps or used in more modern ways – projecting images or a time clock onto a wall, for example.

The relationship of white to these forms of artificial light is crucial – without good lighting, a white room will look dreary and gloomy. 'Good' lighting means ample of all sorts but primarily general (which washes the room with light), task and low-level (concealed, or table and floor lamps) for reading and activities, and spots or kinetic lighting to focus on objects in one or more places around the room.

White is often a starting point in decorating the walls of a room, rather in the nature of a blank canvas. It is a liberating colour – you can start with white and then build on it using other colours, at your own speed,

enjoying the process, perhaps painting one wall at a
time until you have reached the desired degree of
saturation. Starting with white allows you to feel the
power of each individual colour as you add it, at the same
time as watching the colour relationships
developing in your home within a single room or between rooms as you look through from
one to another. Starting with white gives you a term of reference at every stage.

White goes with all the families of colours, freshening them and defining their perimeters,
whether the colour is painted on the wall or provided by other elements such as
fabric or flooring. How fresh and charming a floral print looks, for instance,
when the pink, red or yellow petals and green leaves have a white background. A muted background shade may be effective in another context,
but white is unsurpassed at throwing colours and patterns
into relief.

It is not only on walls and ceilings that white is useful. A white floor may seem
the most impractical decorating idea possible, but given the right circumstances and
treatment it can add a thrilling glamour. If you live several storeys away from the outside
world and have a barrier of doormats (or simply take your outdoor shoes off when you
enter), it is perfectly possible to keep a white-painted floor
clean. A white floor seems to say, 'Practicality is not as important here as
creating a space that is mine, on my own terms, and white is what I want'.
A white floor creates a sense of space and seems to lift everything placed
on it – you almost feel you are floating as you walk across it.

Floor paints have progressed hugely since the days when the only
choice was between red, green or grey industrial products. The best new
paints can in theory be used on concrete, linoleum, cork and vinyl (though you should
patch-test the last three first), as well as on wooden floors without your having to strip
them first. The floor should always be clean, however.

It is also possible to have a whiteish floor that is aesthetically
satisfying, with a bleached driftwood feel, without sacrificing
practicality. Timber boards stripped of all old paint,
varnish or dirt can be painted over (along the grain) with
diluted white emulsion. Once it has been absorbed,
wipe the paint off with a clean cloth so that the grain of the

wood shows through (this method can be used on stripped furniture too), leave to dry then seal it with several coats of **varnish** or hard-wax oil. The look is much like limed wood without your having had the hard work of the traditional method of liming, which involves bringing up the grain with wire wool, rubbing in the wax and then rubbing it off again.

Hard-wax oil is a relatively new product that combines the best features of wax, natural oils and varnish – it is water-repellent like varnish, and oil-based so it seeps into the surface of the wood and flexes with it. Unlike varnish, which creates a totally impervious surface when dry that does not allow for touching up (you have to strip or sand it first), hard-wax oil can be reapplied as necessary in areas of hard wear. It can also be tinted (a milky white among other colours) with proprietary products.

Limed-look or painted floorboards lighten a room and contribute to a contemporary or **Scandinavian style** scheme. They also hark back, interestingly, to the popularity of the **'Moderne' style**. A hallmark of the English designer Syrie Maugham was 'pickled' furniture. Today it would be considered vandalism to strip antique furniture of its polish and patina, but she did just this, finishing the wood anew with pale shades of paint or white wax. The method is a good idea for refreshing undistinguished but attractive or useful items of everyday furniture.

Painting furniture white is a useful trick for the budget decorator. A collection of individual junk-shop finds such as chairs that are to stand round a table will be unified if you paint them all white – or indeed any other colour, but white is plain and simple. Wooden chainstore or high street purchases can be personalized in this way too. Painting rather than aiming for a limed effect will cover up any marks, repairs or other flaws in the wood, and is less labour-intensive since you don't necessarily have to strip the wood first. Any paint designed for use on wood, such as oil-based or **eggshell**, should be sufficiently hardwearing on furniture. If you want to use an oil paint, you may find dead-flat oil paint more pleasing than **gloss.** It is however more porous and will therefore weather or 'distress' more quickly. This may be a desirable effect in itself. Make sure the furniture is clean and not hampered by loose bits of paint or timber before you start work.

The colour white is a theme that runs unbroken through the history of interior decoration, from early interest in formulae that provided good clean tones right into the twenty-first century. Along the way were designers such as Charles Rennie Mackintosh of the Arts and Crafts Movement at the end of the nineteenth century and dawn of the twentieth century. His interiors in Glasgow, Scotland, and elsewhere in Britain used white to create cool spaces for which he designed every piece of furniture and fittings – a far cry from the cluttered, highly patterned and coloured interiors to be found in most homes of the period.

However, the emergence of white paint as an uncompromisingly modern material in interior decoration must be credited to the Modern Movement in the early decades of the twentieth century. This arose out of a feeling among prominent designers, architects, teachers and theorists that a new age required a new attitude to architecture and the applied and decorative arts. The Modern Movement began in continental Europe, but its influence quickly spanned the world and changed architecture and decoration forever.

In America, this clean, sharp, white mode of design was known as the 'International Style' – justifiably so since its architects, such as Edward D. Stone, took it as far afield as Islamabad, Panama and New Delhi, as well as deep-rooting it at home in such seminal structures as Frank Lloyd Wright's Guggenheim Museum in New York. The whiteness of the spiralling white walls of this interior are as much an organic part of it as its unmistakable science-fiction exterior, and they are inextricably linked.

The Modernists rejected ornamentation. Instead they sought to exploit new industrial materials, new uses of traditional materials such as leather, new manufacturing techniques, and new shapes and forms for the exterior and interior of the home and the workplace. The result was a style that was so completely different it was shocking to many, but for others it struck the mood of the moment. Above all, it was modern and impossible to confuse with anything that had gone before.

Among the earliest and most famous buildings to look to us like 'modern' architecture rather than a reinterpretation of the architecture of the past are the sleek, boxy designs of Ludwig Mies van der Rohe, Frank Lloyd Wright and

Charles-Edouard Jeanneret, otherwise known as Le Corbusier. The Villa Savoye (1929–30) at Poissy in France is among Le Corbusier's most visually familiar projects, standing as it does on storey-high legs or *pilotes*, with its flat top and continuous fenestration like a horizontal black stripe turning the corner of the white, concrete building. Le Corbusier was a typical Modernist in believing in only one covering for walls – white paint. Modernism would not be Modernism without plain white walls, even though not all Modernist interiors were white.

Black was the natural balance to white – black leather often supplying support and comfort in furniture designed by Le Corbusier and Charlotte Perriand, his partner. The square upholstered armchairs, the chrome version with leather seats and arms, and the chaise longue they designed have since become design classics, recognizable at a glance. The combination of black and white is always sharp and smart, whether on a chequerboard entrance hall floor in a Georgian mansion or in a contemporary home. Floorboards of uneven colour (perhaps because they have been repaired) look smart and bold painted a deep, glossy black and paired with white walls or a white rug.

In London, Syrie Maugham was creating a highly influential white interior that was utterly different from the hard-edged idealism of Modernism. She took severe white and made it comfortable, luxurious even, by employing expensive, traditional materials and familiar furniture forms. Her drawing room had a silk-covered white sofa (reflected in a mirrored screen) and Louis xv chairs daringly painted white, while the floor was covered with a white rug designed by Marion Dorn. The fashionable artistic circle she inhabited adored it. The drawing room was much-photographed and became one of the decorating icons of the twentieth century. Its style was in complete contrast to the other celebrated influential decorator in vogue in England at the time, Sybil Colefax, whose company, Colefax & Fowler, became a byword for the floral, country house mode of decoration known subsequently as *le style anglais*.

Modernism was in love with white paint, but the thrilling whiteness of modern white paint, the very quality which makes it modern, is a relatively recent achievement. It is due in large part to a pigment which rarely gets a mention in discussion of interior decoration, no doubt partly due to its technical-sounding name: titanium dioxide. This is the 'magic' ingredient in white paint. It is not possible to underestimate the impact that titanium dioxide has had on the interiors of our homes, which makes it all the more extraordinary that it is unfamiliar to a public so fascinated by every practical detail of painting and decorating materials and techniques. Perhaps this is a consequence of interior decoration having become a do-it-yourself industry, not to mention leisure pastime, rather than (as was the case until relatively recently) exclusively for professionals.

Whatever the reason, the distinguishing characteristics of modern paint are opacity and excellent covering power, qualities we take entirely for granted, and these characteristics are attributable to a brilliantly reflective and wonderfully opaque pigment – titanium dioxide – which has revolutionized the performance of paint as we know it.

Titanium dioxide has been known about for centuries but was not exploited or developed until after the Second World War. Its story begins with a country clergyman called William Gregor, who lived in a remote part of England and was interested in minerals. In his spare time he experimented and made chemical analyses of various substances, and in 1791 discovered the element titanium (he called it menaccine) in sand taken from the River Helford. From this he made titanium dioxide. Soon after, a German scientist, Martin Klaproth, made the same discoveries by different means, naming the new mineral 'titanium' after the Titans of Greek mythology. Titanium is now believed to be the planet's ninth most plentiful element.

Today, titanium dioxide is celebrated for its versatility. It is not only used to create modern paints, but also to ensure the dazzling quality of so many coloured materials in the modern world, including plastics, inks, pharmaceuticals, foods and paper – including, no doubt, the pages on which this book is printed. It has many other fine qualities – it is stable and non-volatile, which makes it safe and easy to handle.

Companies in America and Norway led the way in manufacturing titanium dioxide in 1908, believing it had potential, but it was not until after the First World War that it really took off. It was not available in Britain, for example, until 1921. At this stage it was still in a fairly primitive form. In the

1940s a new and better type of titanium dioxide pigment was discovered, made by a different process, and in the 1950s another new idea further enhanced its brilliance. This involved coating each particle of pigment with other materials that, in effect, protected it and made it even more reflective.

A decorating manual of the 1930s, 'The Practical Painter and Decorator', writes in an almost disbelieving tone of the delights of titanium dioxide: 'Of all the white pigments none is equal in opacity and all-round qualities to this most recent addition. It appears,' sighs the author, 'to possess the combined advantages of the other whites without their limitations...' Other white pigments were still listed alongside it, some with intriguing names such as Freemans Non-poisonous White, Chinese White, Antimony White, Natural Barytes, China Clay and Blanc Fixe, in addition to the standard white lead.

White lead had effectively been the pre-eminent white pigment for centuries. One of the reasons why it was eclipsed by titanium dioxide, besides its high cost, was lead's extreme toxicity. Lead paints in general cannot be used today without a special licence, so dangerous are they considered. There is a story about the famous American diplomat Clare Boothe Luce, who became ill while she was USA ambassadress to Italy in the 1950s. Her ailment defied diagnosis until it was discovered that the ceiling of her magnificent palazzo was disintegrating, shedding particles into the air, its historic white lead paint slowly poisoning her.

The measurement of how opaque a pigment is involves gauging not only how much light it reflects, but also how much it absorbs. One of the reasons why titanium dioxide makes such a bright white paint is that is absorbs very little light. It also reflects well, and has what is known as a very high 'refractive index' in water and other solvents. This effect is further enhanced in air, so manufacturers are currently trying to develop ways of keeping air in the paint to make the white brighter still. It is possible that so-called 'brilliant white' may seem relatively dull to us one day.

Historically, as today, paint was a mixture of three or four elements: solvent (to make it liquid), pigment (to give it colour), binder (to glue it all together) and, optionally, an extender to make it go further (and reduce the price). This recipe for paint was true in all parts of the world, from the Americas, across Europe, to Asia and beyond. Paint fell into two distinct types, which still apply today: oil-based and water-based paints. Each type had its advantages and disadvantages, and consequently each its special uses. Whereas today titanium dioxide can be used in any type of paint, historically one of the differences between the two types was the pigments that could be used to create each.

White lead (lead carbonate) was used for making oil-based paints and was sold in different grades that varied considerably in performance as well as cost, but it ceased to be opaque when dissolved in water. Other pigments therefore had to be found. Chalk (calcium carbonate, also known as 'whiting'), gypsum (calcium sulphate) and lime were widely available in Europe and the New World alike for making water-based paints and were much cheaper than lead, but they became transparent in oil so could not be used as pigment in oil-based paints.

Quite apart from the chemistry of paint recipes, the relative whiteness of white, whether it should be tinted with a little lamp black or blue, whether its 'staring, glaring' quality was desirable or not, was a subject of comment at intervals throughout the seventeenth, eighteenth and nineteenth centuries. Although not of pressing importance in comparison to the acquisition of the fashionable colours of the moment and the hugely varying costs of pigments, obtaining effective whites was a constant theme with professional decorators.

Apart from the desirability of achieving white paint as an end in itself, it was needed as a foundation for other colours, which were produced by the addition of coloured pigments. The opacity, or covering power, of these coloured paints was, however, supplied by the white paint base. This is still true to a great extent for modern paints. When you go to a paint supplier and order a paint to be mixed to your choice from the manufacturer's range, pigments are squirted by a machine into a can of the appropriate 'base'. All the bases look like (and are) white paint; what differentiates them is the proportion of white pigment, the base for a dark paint having marginally less than that for a pale shade.

Fascinating as they are, most of the chemical cocktails that constituted paint in past centuries are long gone, but their science and art are increasingly of interest again, both to experts and to ordinary people who consider the decoration of their homes an important matter. There is a general and burgeoning interest in **traditional decorating techniques** that are in sympathy with old buildings.

One of the **types of paint** in which we are interested again, perhaps the most evocative and versatile of all historic white paints, is **limewash**. Not only is it attractive, having a soft, completely matt finish, it is also useful in the decoration of old buildings, especially those whose age or status precludes or avoids the need for a damp-proof course. This is because it is porous, allowing the wall and plaster to breathe, and moisture to escape. As limewash matures, it actually bonds with the plaster behind, if this is lime-based, or with the wall if it has been painted directly onto it.

Paints containing lime have always been considered hygienic and even antiseptic. That this is a fact has recently been confirmed by scientists at the Southwest Research Institute in San Antonio, Texas. They have produced paint which they consider ideal for hospitals because it seems to be deadly to almost all viruses, bacteria and fungi. The paint's key ingredient? Calcium hydroxide, otherwise known as lime.

Limewash is roughly the same concoction across the world, whether used on fishermen's dwellings in Greece, barns and farmhouses in Pennsylvania, and crofters' cottages in the Outer Hebrides or on the coast of Ireland. For centuries, the homes of ordinary working people in countries across the world were (and in some places still are) spruced up annually with several buckets of limewash (or 'whitewash') as part of a 'spring clean' before Whitsun or the festival of Corpus Christi.

Limewash is the most basic material for **sealing plaster** or construction materials such as **brick or stone**, and in past centuries was regularly used to protect the outside of stately buildings as well as homely ones. It is pigment-less, easily made and useful indoors as well as out. To find out more about limewash and how you can make it today, see the *Ideas in Practice* section at the back of the book.

Besides limewash, another basic-sounding paint sometimes mentioned is **'milk paint'**. A more correct name for this is 'casein paint', since casein is the name of the refined protein, extracted from milk when all the lactose and fat have been removed, that acts as the binder in traditional paints. The **Shakers** and early colonial Americans used casein paints stabilized with slaked lime and tinted with earth pigments. Pigment is necessary even if the paint is to be white, since it is transparent without. Casein paint, when dry, gives a resilient finish that can last many years longer than modern paints. In its most basic form, casein paint is simply skimmed milk curd, made by leaving the milk to sour and then straining it to separate the curds from whey, with colour added. If you wanted to make casein paint at home, you could use commercially produced casein powder.

Their matt, chalky finish is one of the most appealing qualities of preparations such as casein paint and limewash. We are used to glossy surfaces on many of the objects around us, from stainless steel pans to chrome furniture and plastic packaging. Even modern matt paints do not have the velvety 'mattness' of old-style paints. This is because they have a type of skin on them since among their ingredients are derivatives of the petrochemical industries (an asset in another context). To see a surface that is not only matt but has a soft depth to it is a rest for the eye and soothing for the soul.

The lovely texture of these natural paints has parallels in other materials and objects that appeal to us – the bark of a silver birch tree, a smooth pebble, the surface of handmade paper. These have an aesthetic quality which, like white itself, hints at a simpler life where we are more in touch with ourselves and with our environment, through contact with natural materials.

OCEAN

WASH

Of all the colours in the rainbow, the most soothing is probably blue. It's the colour of sea and sky – not just any sea and sky, but sunny, fresh, summery sea and sky with their associations of fresh air, relaxation and holidays. Blue is the colour a green landscape becomes as it retreats into the distance and resting your eyes on the horizon gives you a feeling of freedom, space and expansion – room to breathe, space to be yourself. No wonder so many of us want to transport these generous qualities to our living rooms, kitchens, bathrooms and bedrooms.

In some senses, blue has something of a split personality. On the one hand it is a cool, youthful colour – indigo-dyed denim and blue jeans, Mao suits and bleu de travail provide classic images of proletarian liberation and anti-establishment hip. On the other, it speaks of authority, rules and regulations and the ultra-establishment, in the form of school and police uniforms and the obligatory pin-striped suits worn by government officials, city traders and provincial lawyers. Blue can also be grand and even regal, though this is not necessarily desirable if you think of the harsh shade known as 'royal'. As with red, a strong, glowing blue looks stately with gold and silver.

Ironically, pinstripe has broken out, both in fashion terms (well-cut suits for women, in which trousers are of course more subversive than a skirt) and in decorating, where it is seen on upholstery and cushions. Denim, meanwhile, is to be seen upholstering squashy sofas and loose-covered dining chairs, and has even found its way on to our walls as a two-stage paint effect.

As a word, 'blue' has many associations in many different languages. In English, to feel 'blue' is to be sad, 'the Blues' is African-American-inspired music, and to be 'blue with cold' is to be very chilly indeed. Language seems to characterize blue as downbeat. This tallies with the theory of colour psychology, for which blue is intellectual rather than physical. Its influence is reckoned to lower the heartbeat and promote a reflective mood. When the colour moves towards purple, there is an added spirituality.

In terms of interior decoration, mid-blues, especially all shades of powdery sky blue with a reddish tinge, are extremely versatile. As well as working on the walls of any room in the house at any time of day or night, they are fresh in summer and warm in winter. 'Reddish tinge' does not mean that the colour necessarily looks purple (wonderful though purple is), simply that the blue's recipe includes a touch of red pigment which affects its tone very subtly. Other blues can be cool, verging towards grey. Turquoise, which is a greeny blue, is lively and invigorating, a **bright modern colour** with Retro overtones that refer back to 1950s and '60s enthusiasm for formica, the fitted kitchen and daisy prints.

This shade of bright greeny blue also has an immediately recognizable **historic resonance** in the famous glaze achieved on tiles in the medieval Muslim world, still to be seen enlivening mosques and palaces in such countries as Turkey and Iran.

Blue, perhaps more than any other vibrant colour, is truly international. It is as much at home in an **American diner**, paired with shiny silver chrome, or a sedate **Shaker home** as it is painted around the windows of an **Italian farmhouse**, or covering the entire outside of a building in the Indian town of Jodhpur in Rajasthan. Here, blue has the added emotional significance of representing Krishna and mankind's search for enlightenment and ecstasy.

In all its variety, blue works fabulously with white, and brilliant white is the keynote of contemporary decorating. **Blue and white** juxtaposed are fresh and lively, reminding us of Greek islands and Dutch delftware. In the same way that a white shirt worn with denim jeans has become a casual classic of every modern man's and woman's wardrobe, so blue and white always look refreshing together, in any room in the house.

With **neutrals**, those *Desert Shades* described later, blue looks sophisticated and warm. Creams and even soft toffee browns go well with lighter shades of blue, as do greys, both darker and paler. Pale blue looks elegant with almost any colour, including **dark shades of blue** itself.

Team blue with spicy reds, pinks and oranges and it offers a cool note in the same way as green. Yellow and blue are cheerful together and can look sophisticated or childlike, depending on their strength – the paler, the more restrained. **Green and blue** are a delicious combination, whether the tones be soft and gentle or sparkling like emeralds and sapphires.

The 1950s and '60s became the period of the twentieth century when life in the Western world was lightening and brightening after the privations, physical and visual, of the Second World War and its immediate aftermath. Life was, literally, becoming more colourful. Enthusiasm for interior decoration was once again a permissible pleasure after years of austerity. Innovation was not simply acceptable but offered the key to national recovery and a chance for individuals to develop style and taste. Manufacturers of paint could pick up where they left off in the drive for more effective and colourful products.

In the history of decorating, when professionals (known in pre-industrial America as 'colourmen') had to be skilled chemists, mixing their own paint recipes, blue pigments have always been the easiest, presenting relatively few problems. Even if you couldn't afford the very best blue – ultramarine made from ground lapis lazuli (and few could because it was extremely expensive) – there was indigo, smalt, blue verditer, Prussian blue (after about 1710) and from 1828 commercially produced artificial ultramarine. The blues varied in hue, from warm ultramarine, through clean, fresh cobalt and purpley indigo to cerulean blue, which has a green tinge. Prussian blue is a clear blue which makes a delicious sky colour when mixed with white. Its discovery has been hailed as launching the modern pigment manufacturing industry.

In any field of manufacture, industry is always looking for ways of getting ahead of competitors by producing better products that people want. In the world of paint, this striving has been combined with a strong awareness of the health and environmental implications of a material that most people handle and we live with in our own homes.

Oil paints have improved dramatically. Modern paint is still made from the same cocktail of pigment, extender, binder and solvent (pre-industrial paints also sometimes had added resin or varnish). Oil paints, which used to have white spirit or turpentine as a solvent, are now made using a distillate which is safer because it has less powerful fumes and a high flashpoint (the temperature at which it bursts into flames).

In addition to the solvent, the binder, extender and pigment must be considered. Pigments are the chemical equivalents of their historic antecedents. Extenders in both oil and water-based paints are the same as ever: chalk, barytes and china clay, amongst others. The great advance in modern paints is in the binders. Oil paints have as their binder substances derived from soya or sunflower oil, or more unusually, linseed or tung oil. Linseed oil is to be found especially in wood primers, and tung oil in paint for use on wood, where it gives an exceptionally hard finish. The exact ingredients depend on the end use of the paint – there are recipes for industrial paints too, as purely functional protective coats on concrete and steel, for example.

The most distinctive progress in paint in the post-war era, in keeping with the dual themes of customer satisfaction and environmental impact, has been the move away from oil paint towards water-based paints. This could be called the water-based paint revolution.

Some things never change. Modern water-based paints still have as their solvent...water. There have been water-based paints for hundreds, if not thousands, of years – paints such as those we know as distemper and limewash. It is a surprise, therefore, to discover that the new paints did not develop from the old water-based paints but from the new technology in the manufacture of oil paints, which resulted in the creation of vinyls and acrylics. Along with the development of titanium dioxide, vinyls and acrylics have given us the huge range of high-performance water-based paint colours and types from which we can choose today.

Like the natural oils from which they are variously derived, vinyls and acrylics have different qualities that serve different functions. Thus, while vinyls perform well as wall paints, acrylics are used for primers and paints for wood because they stick better to it. PVA (polyvinyl acetate) is the usual vinyl binder for emulsion wall paints – the same PVA, effectively, that makes workshop wood glue and the sticky stuff that children use in school.

As you may have observed from using either of those glues yourself, PVA is milky and matt in the bottle, but dries clear and glossy. Acrylic has the same characteristic. An acrylic gloss paint consequently has a greater proportion of acrylic resin than a matt paint, because it needs the extra to give it a shiny surface. However, because acrylic is clear when dry, the gloss paint is also marginally less opaque. This means that acrylic gloss, with all the advantages of being easy to clean, quick-drying and with a low odour, has the disadvantage of potentially needing more coats for complete opacity. Acrylic gloss is also by its nature slightly less shiny than oil gloss – not necessarily a disadvantage in decorating terms if you prefer its more subtle appearance. The main characteristic in its disfavour is that acrylic gloss shows brushmarks in a way that correctly applied oil gloss does not.

So, what direction will future developments in paint take? The latest trends have included pearlized and metallic finishes and the new generation of floor paints and stains. What is next? This is a question the paint trade is constantly asking itself, manufacturers naturally wanting to be one step ahead of the market. One thought is that, just as today you can go into a DIY store and ask for a specific colour from the range, so one day you will be able to specify one of many slightly **different degrees of shine** (already there are several – silk, sheen and so on) between the extremes of matt and shiny. Each will depend on the proportion of PVA in the paint.

Another area where paint makers are watching for new developments is special **paint effects**. This term used to mean sponging, splattering, stencilling and other fancy surface effects which were in vogue in the 1980s and 1990s. These are still around, but whereas they were once thought by many to be absolute requirements for a fashionable home, they are now viewed more in perspective as options in a range of possibilities. Other options include a textured **marble effect** achieved by applying sheets of tissue paper between coats of paint while the first coat is still wet and stamping patterns rather than stencilling them, over a base coat of plain matt emulsion. For more about the process of **stamping** and the designs that you can create on your walls by this method, see the *Ideas in Practice* section at the back of the book.

One of the features that distinguishes modern water-based paints from their forebears is the wonderful range of additives they contain (though not all at once), each fulfilling a function and improving performance. Compounds can be added to improve the **drying time**, the flow of the paint or the thixotropic quality of the paint (the 'tomato ketchup' effect which makes it thick and gelatinous rather than completely liquid – good for ceiling paints, for example). Some paints include an anti-skinning agent, which evaporates to fill out the space between the top of the paint and the lid of the tin to prevent oxidization; some paints have a bacticide to stop bugs and bacteria growing in the paint.

Another important function of **chemical additives** is to render the paint anti-fungal and preservative, giving it an extended shelf life before the tin is opened and for some time afterwards. Anti-fungals are also added to paints for **kitchens and bathrooms** where the atmosphere is likely to be damp. Because of additives like these, modern water-based paints can be used in places such as bathrooms where before only oil paints were suitable. Today's water-based paints give a completely waterproof, hardwearing, washable surface when dry.

The move towards water-based paint has many benefits. In the factory, the manufacture of these paints is more **environmentally friendly**, generates fewer health and safety restrictions, and (as at home) the material is easier and more pleasant to handle. Water-based paints are also less inflammable, which has positive implications also for transport and retailing. Such was the danger from the 'old style' oil paints and varnishes that a factory was required to have separate buildings around the yard for pigment making, shellac manufacture (this required the use of methylated spirit) and the production of the paint itself. In the case of a fire, at least it could theoretically be contained in one area only.

A small irony of our love of paint appears when you consider distressed painted furniture in which the effect of age and wear can be created using the newest and best modern paints. There is something uniquely appealing about a piece of country furniture that has been coated with layer upon layer of paint to protect it and keep it smart over the years, yet the paint has worn away in places where the piece is often touched. This wearing-away occurs especially around handles and knobs, and on corners and obtruding edges. Furniture painted today can acquire a similarly attractive patina of age and experience naturally over time, but the **aged look** can also be purposely recreated with modern water-based (or indeed oil) paints.

The simplest method of achieving a **distressed look** is to paint a piece with layers of different coloured paint – shades of the same colour are discreet, with the darker colour underneath for best effect. Once this is dry, simply buff with sandpaper the places that would naturally get wear and tear, starting with a coarse grade and progressing to a finer grade. Another method involves using an old candle to wax over the darker layer of paint in places where you want it to show through, and sanding or scraping these after the lighter layer has dried. You can also devise your own methods, doing clever things with beeswax and turpentine or artists' masking fluid. A final buff with **antiquing wax** can help the appearance of age. Paint is wonderfully compliant stuff and the distressed effect is not difficult to achieve.

FOREST
HUES

Green is the colour we associate above all with nature. Autumn may be rife with browns, reds and golds but green is an all-year-round colour, a perennial. Its tones vary, of course, from season to season and depending where you are in the world. In the tropics, greens come alive in the rainy season. In winter in the northern hemisphere there is less green on trees, but grass is luxurious, well-fed and springy. In England, spring is green's high festival, its brightness and lushness unequalled. Summer is verdant too, but only until the heat of the sun has scorched lawns and dust settles on hills and hedgerows.

The amount of green you see out of your window depends whether you live in a city or the country, and in a temperate or arid zone. To see some rather than none, however, is good for your health. Looking at trees really is beneficial. They provide a focus outside ourselves, they lift the eye from our immediate tasks and they lift the soul. Trees have variety and movement, they provide an ever-shifting picture of life on earth – en masse or singly, they draw the eye and soothe us.

The ancient oriental science of feng shui recognizes the meditational quality of the colour green. More than any other colour, green is tranquil. In the body, it is linked to the heart; in the psyche and in life, to balance and symmetry; in all aspects, green is associated with growth, as you might expect. Too much green, however, and its effect becomes negative – relaxation becomes something akin to apathy.

Indoors, green must be handled with care. Some shades of green may not always reflect well on human skin, unlike warmer reds, oranges, yellows and browns. Green seems to retreat from us, keeping its distance. This is ideal for living rooms or hallways that have plenty of traffic, rather than bedrooms and bathrooms.

Green has always been a popular colour for interior decorating. Green of one shade or another is almost invariably in fashion. The names alone of various shades of green are poetic, tantalizing – names such as duck egg, sea green, *eau de nil*, verdigris, apple, mint, acid and Provençal. The current favoured tones are soft sage or celadon, the misty tone you see on glazed oriental pottery, and a light leafy green that is fresh and juicy. At one time lime green was in vogue, often used with bright violet or tangerine but fashions change and these combinations were later considered a little too harsh, perhaps a little lacking in subtlety.

In decorating, the great advantage of green is that there is a shade of it to go with every other colour. It is the perennial best friend, available to chaperone the most wayward hue or to uplift the most subdued (shades of blue have a similar quality). Soft greens go well with other gentle tones that are popular – greys, taupe, mauve, chalk white, dusty pink. Fresh, more yellow greens can cool down the most exotic cocktail of jangling pinks and oranges, enliven a palette of neutrals or simply be funky without looking girlie, set against brilliant white. Above all, green-painted walls give us a sense of being in touch with nature, bringing a breath of freshness into the home.

Like green, yellow is generally used to paint the walls of kitchens (where it is bright and warm without becoming over-heated) and living rooms, rather than bedrooms and bathrooms. Certain shades of yellow do not reflect well on humanity in the early morning, though warmer, oranger tones can be enlivening. Mellow yellow is easy to live with – a soft, mustardy mayonnaise colour is warm and welcoming without lacking character. Pale yellows tend to be a trifle chilly. A bedroom with bright yellow walls will feel sunny but not necessarily restful. Traditionally (and in feng shui), colour theory considers yellow to be invigorating and intellectual while its warmer orange cousin is less cerebral and more sociable.

Floors also benefit from the liveliness of green. A polite sage tone has been considered a useful carpet colour for decades, but painting a floor is a much more versatile option. It will seal the floor of a kitchen or bathroom and make it waterproof, it will give a coloured background to rugs and throw them into relief and there is a huge choice of colours to contribute to your overall scheme. Most paint ranges now include a wide choice of floor paints, as manufacturers have realized their decorating potential. If you can't find the exact shade you want in a floor paint, you can resort to painting it with your choice of eggshell paint, giving it several coats, followed by a couple of varnish coats for added protection.

An inexpensive alternative, if you don't have a wooden floor to paint, is to colour cork tiles. A hard-wax oil will do this, as will most good floor paints, the only prerequisite being that the tiles have not been pre-sealed. You can also stain or paint floor tiles made of some other material, such as MDF (medium-density fibreboard), either in a traditional chequerboard of two colours or by using more colours in a random pattern for a contemporary rather than a classic look. Even vinyl can take a coat of paint once it has been prepared using one of the new generation of specialist primers.

The **range** of fresh and bright greens we take for granted are a mid-twentieth-century invention. Chemical pigments are manufactured by specialist companies, which supply them not only to paint factories but to the makers of every imaginable coloured product we use in our homes and our lives. Typically, a manufacturer of paint will make an entire range of dozens, if not hundreds, of paints from only sixteen or twenty bought-in powdered or liquid pigments used in a bewildering number of combinations and quantities. In dramatic contrast, the early green pigments created a very limited range of tones that were earthy in character. The best known is a natural pigment made from the mineral glauconite and is actually called *terre verte* (green earth), which is exactly what it is.

A wide range of copper-based substances was used to create the green pigments of **history**. Some proved more satisfactory than others. Most often used, until the eighteenth century, were verdigris (better in oil) and green verditer (better in water-based paint such as distempers). Neither was ideal, though both were commonly used in house decoration. Verdigris gave a soft, blueish tone; green verditer a fresher shade. A disadvantage of verdigris was that it would blacken when in contact with carbon dioxide and other gases in the air. Other pigments such as sap green and malachite (literally crushed malachite) were available but hardly used.

The first serious alternative to verdigris and green verditer was copper chloride Brunswick **green**, made by the Gravenhorst brothers in Brunswick in 1764 and followed soon after by 'distilled' Brunswick green (better but more expensive). Other firms sold similar green pigments for making paint, under such names as English verdigris, Bremen green and patent green. Another useful green was emerald (copper aceto-arsenite), available from 1816 onwards, but this had several operational drawbacks. It was highly toxic, it turned brown when damp and it could not be used near pigments containing sulphur. The accomplished decorator or colourman had also to be an amateur chemist in order to master his trade.

The great breakthrough in making stable, lively green paint colours came with the discovery not of a green pigment but of a yellow – **chrome yellow**. Historian Ian Bristow called this dazzling, intense colour 'the pigment for which the eighteenth century had been waiting'. The eighteenth century – but only just. Chromium, the element, was discovered in 1798 and by the early years of the nineteenth century was being extracted at Pennsylvania and Maryland in America and Var in France. Chrome yellow was established as the height of fashion by its use in the music room at Brighton Pavilion, England, in 1818.

In earlier ages, yellow pigments based on lead were known in Egypt and Mesopotamia. They were used in artists' oil paints in various forms, including lead tin yellow, naples yellow (a lead antimonate) and patent yellow (lead oxychloride). Patent yellow provided the paint for the famous first-floor drawing rooms at Sir John Soane's house in Lincoln's Inn Fields, London, in 1812. The other prestigious yellow paint was king's yellow, a purified sulphide of arsenic. As well as being poisonous, however, this did not wear well, tending to become speckled. It smelt unpleasant and was incompatible with pigments containing copper or lead. By comparison, chrome yellow was relatively trouble-free, although poisonous.

'Chrome yellow Brunswick green' is a mouthful of a name for a pigment in its own right – considered such because blue is added during the making of the yellow rather than afterwards (when it tends to separate and is, in any case, not such a bright colour).

Strong colours such as this were prestigious on account of their novelty, as well as the fact that bright colours are uplifting to live with. They also tended to be expensive, paints with saturated tones costing more than deep colours and being considerably more expensive than paints based on earth pigments or needing only a touch of pigments such as Prussian blue to give them variety. Green as a decorating colour was consistently popular throughout the eighteenth and nineteenth centuries, though different tones held sway at different times and in different places.

Homewood House in Baltimore, the United States, famous as a fine and charming example of a prosperous eighteenth-century home, provides an example of the popularity and impact of pea green. This delicious vegetable tone manages to be both fresh and mellow at the same time. Copper-based pigments provided pea green and also the various blues with which the house is decorated. In northern Europe, meanwhile, in the first half of the nineteenth century a chrome-based, brilliant green was popular with the Biedermeier style of furniture and decoration. Bieder is German for 'unpretentious', and the style has a refreshing simplicity of line combined with a sophistication, which is the consequence of using fine, golden woods and elegant detailing. Bright colours were a vital part of the Biedermeier style, none more so than emerald green.

In Britain a few years later, Queen Victoria and her German husband Prince Albert were popularizing everything Scottish, especially tartan. Tartan fabric, tartan carpet, tartan sashes...the colour most common to all of these being green. Modest city houses picked up on these colours, using rich, jewel-like tones (at least until sullied by pollution), including shades that we would call bottle green and racing green.

There was plenty of green in the last decades of the nineteenth century and early decades of the twentieth. The creators of popular operetta, Gilbert and Sullivan, made fun of Aubrey Beardsley and the 'Aesthetic' set with their reference to 'greenery yallery' in their operetta *Patience*, and the term quickly became a cynical catchphrase for pretentious, effeminate artiness. The sinuous lines of Art Nouveau took their inspiration from plant and flower forms, so a limpid green was their obvious choice of tone. Members of the Arts and Crafts Movement, meanwhile, had been experimenting with natural dyes and pigments, which resulted in the range of rich greens and ochres familiar in the wallpaper and textile designs of the hugely influential designer William Morris. These carried over into painted interiors of the period such as that at Standen in Sussex, England, built for the Beale family by Philip Webb and now opened to the public by the National Trust.

In the context of the Art Nouveau and Arts and Crafts movements, the colour green tinged the interiors and exteriors of buildings across the world in the early decades of the last century. From Victor Horta's organic interiors such as the Hotel Tassel in Brussels, with its green columns growing out of the floor and into the ceiling, to the influential interiors of the great Frank Lloyd Wright, shades of green are at home. Wright's Storer House in Los Angeles does not seem at first glance to be more one colour than another – it simply looks natural, with its wooden floors, ceilings and stone walls. Look more closely and you will see that the upholstery is pale green, the ceramics celadon, the patterned leather edging on wooden bucket chairs has a mossy hue and the tiffany-style glass lamp has deep emerald glass. These tones are an organic part of the whole.

Decorating a Georgian or Victorian house in a style in keeping with its age has hardly been easier since the period itself. The upsurge in interest for historic paints has caused the re-emergence of a kaleidoscope of shades both rich (suitable for mid- to late-nineteenth-century homes) and delicate (better suited to earlier, Georgian houses, except where you wish to emulate the homes of the very wealthy who could afford stronger and brighter pigments). Most ranges are available either from DIY and decorating chainstores or by mail order; in specialist paint shops the staff are often highly knowledgeable and will sometimes even advise on exact colours. Paint finishes, too, are more varied than they have been for decades. Distemper, with its lovely matt surface, is on the menu once more after being almost completely out of production since the 1970s because of today's huge upsurge of interest in types of paint sympathetic to old buildings.

Distemper is a water-based paint containing no petrochemical derivatives. Once it was an almost universal sealant and decorative finish, and not only in the homes of people of modest means. The Queen's drawing room and privy chamber at Whitehall Palace in London were painted with it in 1674 – doors, window woodwork, shutters, panelling and all. It was not confined to walls and timber, but was also used to stain parquet flooring and porous tiles. The latter were given several coats of paint and oil, then finished off with topcoats of polished wax.

Ceilings too were distempered, in coloured paint as well as white, from around the middle of the eighteenth century, as were plaster walls that sometimes had paper pasted on to them, over which the paint was applied. Sometimes the distemper was simply a curing coat – a paint film that could be applied to protect new plaster, through which it could dry until it was brushed or washed off a couple of years later in order for the plaster to be redecorated with an oil paint. This new paintwork might be washed but such was the cost of paint, especially in early America with its transport challenges, that once an oil paint had been applied that room might never be decorated again.

The porosity of distemper, the way that it allows the wall beneath to breathe, is one of its most appealing qualities to today's owners and custodians of old buildings if they want to decorate them appropriately, in keeping with their age and mellow appearance. Modern paints, by contrast, tend to seal the wall behind a plastic film.

A manual dating from about 1811 gives some common sense directions as to the best method of applying distemper – quickly and evenly. On ceilings, 'Lay it all one way, and that from the light to the dark part of the room, always beginning on the window side'. Walls were sometimes varnished after distempering, which increased the wear it could take but must have virtually eliminated its valuable porosity.

Paint primarily consists of pigment, which gives it colour, solvent (in the case of distemper, this is water) and a binder, which effectively holds it together so that you can spread it on the wall. The original binder for distemper was 'size', a glue made from boiling animal skin, horn and bone in water. The more refined the animal parts, the finer the size, one of the best being made from shreds of glove leather or ink-free parchment parings. The air bladder of the sturgeon was reputed to make the finest possible size, but this must have been a rare commodity indeed.

As early as the late 1820s, manufacturers were experimenting with emulsions (tiny drops of oil suspended in water) and this led to the development of 'washable' distempers. Emulsion paints as we know them today, using petrochemicals, were not produced in commercial quantities until after the Second World War, but by the 1970s emulsions had taken over in both America and Britain.

Production may have all but ceased, but interest in paints such as limewash and distemper never died. Experts in old buildings knew their value and persisted in using them, and a few traditional manufacturers retained the facilities and the knowledge of how to produce distemper commercially. Those who did, smaller firms rather than the giants, were in a position to offer an updated version of distemper when historic building organizations led the way in marketing it in the 1990s as a vehicle for colours in sympathy with old buildings. The appeal of the colours, the breathable quality of distemper (even modern distemper) and the depth of matt finish go hand in hand and are the reasons for the dramatic increase in demand.

Distemper made today is recognizably the same type of product as before, but there are differences. It still consists of the same basic elements, but the extenders are usually barium sulphide and chalk, which help to give it the desirable dusty matt finish that responds so attractively to changes in the quality of natural light.

The pigments used in distemper have and haven't changed. Some are earth pigments, which would be recognized by a master decorator two centuries ago when it was (as now) dug out of the ground and refined as locally to the paint factory as possible. Others are modern chemical pigments, which are used to achieve the desired colours with much greater stability than before, and also better consistency and reliability. Contemporary consumers may rejoice in the appeal of distemper, but they also expect the paint to perform.

One other difference in the pigmentation of paints is the use of titanium dioxide. Although it is only used in very small quantities to produce distemper today, nonetheless it is used by some manufacturers and gives paler colours their opacity. Its main importance in the manufacture of paints approximating to historic recipes is as a replacement for white lead in oil paint.

A difference between contemporary paints and historic colours is that a greater number of pigments is generally used to devise a historic range. This is because historic paints typically included a larger proportion of stronger and deeper colours than a modern range of paint shades does. Deeper shades, especially reds, can suffer from a lack of opacity because less titanium dioxide (known for its brilliant whiteness and therefore less suitable in this context) is used.

Other differences between today's distemper and historic paints are almost entirely in favour of today's decorator. Historic paints would not have been as smooth as modern paints, having tiny particles and impurities introduced by any one of their ingredients, as well as the atmosphere in which they were made. They would have been more difficult to apply with an even finish, without getting blemishes or slight changes in colour (the equivalent in historic oil paint was called 'flashing', when slightly glossier patches would appear) and they would have taken longer to dry.

The binders used today are commercially produced equivalents to those of old, primarily casein and size. Casein was used almost exclusively in a domestic context to make paints at home; size was used by professionals. Casein is particularly useful today as it can be blended with emulsified oils to make washable or oil-bound distempers (or 'oil-bound water paint', as it should strictly be called). These are harder wearing than soft distempers and make the paint acceptable to the modern householder – soft distemper rubs off on your clothes and furniture. In previous centuries this was considered normal and the wall would simply be brushed or washed down every year or so, and a new coat of paint applied. We expect more from a paint today, even a historical one. Oil-bound distemper cannot only be rubbed, but also lightly washed. The only disadvantage of casein is that it does not stay fresh indefinitely, so the paint's shelf life and the time it will be usable at home are therefore limited.

Colour consistency has been achieved to a much greater extent between batches of today's historic paints, but it is still not infallible. Just as in previous centuries, you are well advised to use paint from only one batch when decorating a room in order to avoid even tiny colour differences. Be generous when calculating the quantity of paint you need so that you will not run out. Another tip to help avoid colour problems is never to finish a tin of paint. Always add some of the next tin (having stirred it first) to the bottom inch or so of the last and mix it well before using it, even if both tins came from the same batch.

EARTH
TONES

'The red-brown

most magnific

have the powe

sensual conne

same time as

us to comfort

fantasy lands

hues of the
ent chocolate
 to evoke
tions, at the
ransporting
ng childhood
.. ,

Chantal Coady, Rococo Chocolates

Of all the colour families, none is more down-to-earth (literally) than the earth tones. Earth, from which all life-sustaining nourishment issues, is brown. Not dirty, sludgy brown, but the enriching colours of soil in all its planet-wide variety. Earth tones range from peaty loam so rich it is almost black, through the yellows and terracottas of packed clay soil, to startling bright orangy red and a million variations inbetween.

Earth tones are the most deeply sensual of all the families of colour. Their names roll round the tongue so deliciously they seem good enough to eat. You can almost smell them, too. Bitter chocolate, mocha, milky coffee, fudge, bark, wood, oatmeal, biscuit (the last two perhaps belong in the *Desert Shades* chapter by virtue of their paleness), pumpkin, Seville orange, Burgundy, aubergine and plum.

These earthy colours embrace us physically with their visual warmth. They have associations that wrap us up with a sense of security. The colour of blood is, after all, the colour of the womb whence we all sprang, innocent and free of fear. Deep red tones seem therefore to be reassuring; they make us feel centred and belonging. They have a primeval appeal. We know where we are with them – safe.

Nature is brim-full of reds, ochres and browns, especially in autumn and winter: berries in the hedgerows; ripe apples and pears on the trees; the mottled bark of tree trunks (each species with its own tones) and the colour of leafless branches and twigs, their sap low, their colours darkened by rain and fallen leaves mound up on the ground below in piles of gold, orange and brown, sometimes ruby red, scrunchy and brittle.

Nuts, glossy and inviting hazelnuts or coarse-shelled walnuts and Brazil nuts; horse chestnuts sitting fatly in their white fleshy coverings, burst open to reveal the polished brown-maroon treasure within; rosehips, some round and juicy-looking, some slender and elegant; crab apples hanging heavy, weighing down supple branches; bright red berries on holly and pyrocanthus; rusty beech leaves like so much crushed paper in the hedges, refusing to blow away until defeated by spring gusts... The images of autumn have a rustic beauty, but they also make us want to wrap up, to retreat to the comfort of our homes, to light a fire and gather round it, to stare into the dancing flames and agitate the embers, to share hot-buttered toast and muffins with family and friends, perhaps a glass of spiced wine or a hot toddy, to light candles after dark.

Brown as a **decorating colour** is far from being dull. On the contrary, shades such as bitter chocolate are once again appreciated for themselves, especially now that they are divorced from the shrill oranges and yellows which so often accompanied them in the 1970s. Today, browns both **velvety matt** and **sleekly glossy** are smart and sexy. They live happily with other earth tones such as ruby and russet, and with **paler shades** such as sand and pearly greys. Browns look rich with creamy whites and sharp with brilliant white or shades of chalk and milk. Like all dark colours, bitter chocolate looks fabulous but is an impractical colour in decorating. This makes it all the more desirable and sophisticated, but it is not recommended for those with children or pets.

In an age when we have all become more aware of the sympathy, or otherwise, of our homes and our lives to the environment, it is not surprising that there has been such a strong resurgence of interest in **'natural' and historic** paints. These are perceived as being more in tune with location and the age of a building than modern products. In the 1990s, various manufacturers used the 'heritage' label to market paint colours in groups such as **'Georgian'** and **'Victorian'** (the latter being particularly strong in rich earth tones), in order to guide the consumer (us) in finding a certain style or to decorate our homes appropriately according to their age.

Distinguished organizations such as the Victoria & Albert Museum and the National Trust in Britain linked up with commercial companies, using their expertise to produce paints that are not only **appropriate colours** for old buildings, but are also made to recipes that are in sympathy with the structure, in the form of distempers and even limewash. In America, too, there is keen interest in the heritage of paint manufacture (which mirrors that in Europe) and in using paints sympathetic to old buildings. These products have fulfilled consumer demands but have also themselves generated huge interest, with the result that paints with historic resonance are now firmly re-established on the market after so many decades of neglect. Even their names are appealingly atmospheric, with reds and browns sporting titles such as Bengal Rose, Pompeian Red, Better Class Red, Dragon's Blood Red and Warm Sepia.

One of the reasons for the success of these paints is that their colours and soft matt finishes are, frankly, ravishing. The reds and pinks are sumptuous, their richness and life-enhancing warmth a pleasure to live with. Their matt quality is appealing, responding as it does to changes in the quality of daylight, as well as looking equally handsome by artificial light. An ordinary room suddenly looks special when dressed in one of these earthy tones. They are such a decorating asset that, once experienced, we wonder how we ever did without them. In old buildings especially, for which they were of course designed, these colours seem completely relaxed. They belong; they are as much at home in an ancient stone farmhouse in the Yorkshire Dales as in a converted barn in New Jersey, in an Edinburgh townhouse as in a Texan ranch house. They are distant but distinct relations of paints that have never been out of use in Mexico, Marakesh and Malegaon.

Earth tones reflect well on old beams and polished wooden floors; antique furniture shows up well against them, and so do the gilt frames of pictures and mirrors. When you enter a room decorated in this way you feel you are making an entrance. Browns, reds and pinks work well in any room where you are going to sit for any length of time, such as a living room or dining room (if you have such a room – they are rarer now than they once were). Lighter shades are fine for a kitchen or playroom, or for a bedroom. The advantage these pinks have over many modern tones is that they are mellow – soft but sufficiently robust never to be sugary.

Earth tones, whether in the form of historic or modern paints, are also ideal for small and potentially chilly spaces such as stairwells and lavatories. An entrance hall painted a vigorous earthy shade says 'welcome' to visitors, and embraces you every time you return to it. These colours also work well in dark rooms – much better than a pastel shade or white, which make a dark room seem gloomy and cold.

Browns and reds are equally at home in a contemporary decorating scheme as they are in a historic one. In an older house decorated in sympathy with its age, earth tones work in harmony with greys, browns and possibly some deep shades of blue, green and yellow. In a modern scheme any one of these colours will act as an anchor to a wide range of light, floaty hues.

A warm, nutty brown goes well with voilets, mauves and light purples such as lavender. It also adds

122

warmth to cooler tones of grey and light blues. It can work with fresh, pale shades of green – beware sludgier shades, which can look a trifle depressing with brown. It works least well with **yellows and oranges**, with which it can look uncomfortable (black works better here, or grey). It also looks stunning with **white and neutrals**.

Reds, pinks and oranges (separately, or even all at once) can provide highlights in a neutral or white interior, and at the same time add warmth. **Coloured glass** is effective in this way, especially if placed in a window, where changing natural light will result in patches of colour moving around the room. **Cushions** and throws will introduce warm accents to a white room, while a stronger focus can be provided by a large-scale warm-toned **rug** on the floor or a **wallhanging**. The latter could be a rug, a textile such as a kimono or ethnic garment, a poster or a picture.

Pale tones of earth colours make a sympathetic background for richly coloured objects – a collection of hats or wooden hat moulds, for example, hung in a pattern on the wall. In a **kitchen**, wooden and ceramic bowls can be arranged along an open shelf where they can be seen and enjoyed, as well as being easily accessible for use.

Metallic and pearly paints are not only made in neutrals and pale cool tones. Paints with bronze and gold glittery finishes are also available, and will add interest and a touch of glamour to an interior decorated in earthy shades.

However, the element that has traditionally introduced brown into the decoration and furnishing of our homes is, of course, **wood**. That most reassuring of materials has also for hundreds of years been a vital necessity for the construction of houses great and small. Its strength when seasoned is indubitable – indeed, most countries count timber-framed buildings among their finest and most popular forms of heritage, many having stood for more than half a millennium.

We now largely use **stone**, **brick** and **concrete**, but there is still a demand for timber-framed houses, for several reasons. They are practical, economical and environmentally friendly, with satisfying proportions. Where the massive timbers are visible, as in green-oak barns, the wood is beautiful and the engineering of the building's beams and trusses a feast for the eye. Not only is the wood appealing when new and 'green', it becomes more beautiful with age. Another element which gives us deep satisfaction when we contemplate such vernacular buildings is the almost tangible sense of workmanship involved in making them – the pride of the workmen who hewed the wood and fitted the pieces together.

Wooden floors, too, are no longer viewed as the draughty eyesore they were considered by the post-war generation, for whom obliteration with fitted carpets was the ideal treatment. Draughts can still be a problem but not an insurmountable one, any more than splinters or patches of repair. Industrial sanding machines are now readily available from hire centres, and a wonderful range of sealants, including the latest generation of tinted acrylics and microporous wax-oils, has transformed the wooden floor into a desirable decorative element.

Wooden 'trim' (as it is known in the paint industry) consists of the skirting board, architrave or other framing around the doors and windows, the door jambs and frames, the windowsills, and any other timber edging such as a dado or picture rail. These timber pieces are necessary where a surface of one material meets another, to cover the join and provide a rigid straight edge, desirable for both aesthetic and practical terms.

These edging pieces are invariably made of softwood such as pine and are almost as invariably painted (usually white), or at least protected with a sealant. In previous periods the colour and finish of interior woodwork have gone through various vogues, including shades of flat brown which imitated its natural colour and didn't show dust and soot, and decorative woodgraining. Today, skirting boards and door jambs painted a colour other than white or the colour of the walls add character and definition and give you the opportunity to develop a colour combination or relationship begun elsewhere in the room. For some practical information on painting wood see *Ideas In Practice*.

The painting of wood has changed hugely since the Victorian age, when at least six exhaustive stages were recommended. Today, an acrylic undercoat makes short work of the preparation, but decorators still prefer oil-based paints or acrylic eggshell for the top coat as acrylic gloss shows brushmarks.

Woodgraining, the decoration of surfaces in imitation of the grain of fine and hard woods, has a long and distinguished pedigree. From the seventeenth century onwards, householders expected a qualified house decorator to be able to imitate a range of timbers and marbles in important rooms, in order to disguise the humble reality of the cheaper timbers used to construct affordable doors, fireplaces and panelling.

The styles of graining that a master decorator could offer in the nineteenth century, after the introduction of new techniques, was even more impressive. It included specific species of trees – mahogany, for example, in both its Spanish and Honduras strains, both a rich reddish brown. Equally specific but (to us) less familiar woods were also imitated – for example, pencil cedar (pinkish with reddish lines), amboyna (nut-brown and whorled) and olive wood (light brown with a greenish tinge, and finely veined). American cherry, a yellowish wood with a pretty, delicate grain, was another option. The history of woodgraining is a fascinating subject in itself.

When the fashion for chinoiserie appeared at the very beginning of the nineteenth century, bamboo became especially popular. In England, the Prince Regent made the Chinese style fashionable, decorating the Royal Pavilion in Brighton in a riot of orientalism. The salon alone required thousands of square feet of imitation bamboo, while elsewhere even fireplaces and iron balusters were decorated to look as if they were made of sticks of bamboo.

The pigments that make earth tones in paint are the ones that, literally, come out of the ground and are consequently known as the earth pigments. That this has made them predominant the world over for thousands of years we know since the discovery of the caverns at Lascaux in France, decorated by cave dwellers, and they were probably used even earlier. These pigments are the ochres, siennas and umbers. The last two derive their names from the places whence they came historically, Siena and Umbria in Italy.

Raw umber, burnt sienna, yellow ochre...the names are familiar from artists' colours and therefore have an appealingly Bohemian ring to them. Raw umber pigment is in fact strong in manganese and is therefore a relatively cool dark brown. Burnt umber is made from heating the raw form, resulting in a warmer, redder shade. Raw sienna has less manganese and the clay from which it is made is therefore less dark brown (more of a brownish orange colour). Burnt sienna is darker and redder, and makes attractive shades of pink when diluted with white.

Like all pigments, earth pigments vary in degrees of opacity or transparency. The one that consistently gives the best covering power is yellow ochre. It doesn't tend to fade much, though some degree of fading is one of its charms (at least until you try to patch up a wall from a fresh batch of paint). Raw and burnt sienna are less opaque, and the umbers less still, but their light permanence is good (they don't fade). The umbers' relatively poor opacity makes them ideal for woodgraining and other paint effects which involve layer upon layer of semi-transparent glaze.

Ochres contain no manganese, the tone of the pigment resulting from the presence of iron oxide, which also contributes to the colour of the umbers and siennas. Red pigments based on red ochre go under various names, including Indian red, Mars red, Persian earth and Prussian red, each one a slightly different colour and with a different history. Yet another pigment, Venetian red (now produced artificially) is a more vibrant shade of red than the siennas and umbers can offer, on account of containing (originally) as much as forty per cent iron oxide.

Iron oxide is, effectively, rust. It occurs naturally in rocks and soil all round the world from which natural earth pigments are extracted, and is the reason for so many wonderful browns, reds and oranges. Because iron oxide pigments, containing varying amounts of other minerals such as manganese, are available virtually out of the ground in so many geographic locations, they have always been cheap and plentiful. This is why they are used on vernacular buildings, inside and out, and as a result the buildings become literally part of the landscape. This is part of the appeal of vernacular architecture as well as of local pigments.

In the nineteenth century, it was not only buildings that were coloured with earth pigments – animals and people were too, or men of one particular trade, at least. Thomas Hardy describes one of a breed that was dying even then in *The Return of the Native*, published in 1878.

The old man (the first person we meet in the novel) saw:

a spring van, ordinary in shape, but singular in colour, this being a lurid red. The driver walked beside it; and, like his van, he was completely red. One dye of that tincture covered his clothes, the cap upon his head, his boots, his face, and his hands. He was not temporarily overlaid with the colour: it permeated him.

The old man knew the meaning of this. The traveller with the cart was a reddleman – a person whose vocation it was to supply farmers with redding for their sheep.

Within living memory, farmers in Cumbria in the north-west of England reddened their Herdwick sheep for show. The traditional way of keeping track of which ewes the ram had tupped at breeding time was to paint the ram's belly red – a different shade each week so that you knew which ewes would give birth when.

Other earthy-coloured pigments also occur naturally, but are either so rare, so toxic or so difficult to extract that they were used much less than the iron oxide pigments. They also tended to be used by the **specialist painter** rather than by locals living on the land, looking for a finish to help protect their homes from the elements (protection being one of the main purposes of paint). These pigments include a sulphide of arsenic known as red orpiment or realgar, red lead and vermilion (red lead being more orange than vermilion). So expensive were these last two, and so effective, that they tended to be used to tint paint colours first obtained more cheaply by using umbers and siennas, rather than as individual colours on their own. Red lead was also, of course, highly toxic. Today's paints largely protect users, both professional and otherwise, from such poisonous side effects, but they have nonetheless been developed by building on the discoveries of previous ages.

DESERT SHADES

The family of colours this chapter celebrates are those restful tones we see in string and old stone, hay and straw, sun-dried shells and sand – namely, the desert shades. Far from inhabiting an arid, infertile plain, however, these colours provide a positive feast of subtle choices – subtle rather than startling, *piano* rather than *forte*. The family encompasses warmer shades and cooler ones, from clotted cream to gritty grey – all discreet but none lacking their own quiet character. All evocative.

Consider grey – the colour of mist. Soft and hazy hues seen in very early morning light, when the birds are barely awake. That romantic time when the dew lies heavy, dreams still seem real and there is leisure to stretch and anticipate. There is no rush at the grey moment of the morning – the day seems to stretch ahead endlessly, lazily...

In nature, desert shades give us the colour of pebbles on the beach, some streaked with white, black or pink, the worn-out tones of driftwood and bright, translucent spray. Pearls are one of the sea's greatest treasures, lustre beyond price. Other tones remind us of seagulls' eggs and their wings, or of lichen on old stone.

Some desert tones are darker than others, the colours of cool shadows that grow deeper as the heat of the day fades away. Bluish slate, silvery pewter, deep charcoal...the greys that have depth and resonance, that remind us of rain on cobbles. These are serious greys, offering an alternative to black in a chic woman's wardrobe; they go so well (better than black) with red, cream, lilac and all the other delicious colours in which you can envelop yourself with a pashmina.

Grey is a colour of infinite variety, but as well as being among the most sensuous and subtly splendid it also gets a bad press. Grey days are dreary, a 'grey' mood signifies depression, and grey is the non-colour of so much utilitarian 'stuff ' – the plastic casing of computers, chicken wire, concrete urban wastelands. A woman whose hair turns grey is still (by some) expected to be ashamed, to cover the grey with dye, whilst grey hair on a man is appealing, a signal of life lived, of maturity. But times change. Grey hair is now elegant. Even makers of hair colouring celebrate grey in a range of special tints.

Grey is a distinguished member of this family of desert shades that also includes the neutrals – tones that have been rediscovered in recent decades as perhaps having a charm of their own when used in interior decoration.
They are discreet, unchallenging, the ultimate comfortable colours. Used with plenty of variety of texture such as sheepskin, tweed,

ceramic and blond wood (which their restraint allows you to notice and enjoy), neutrals can be supremely sophisticated.

Neutrals and soft, ethereal hues help us to aspire to an uncomplicated existence, to coolness and calm, an absence of clutter. Tones of buttermilk and orchid, basket and shell epitomize the natural home and the simple life. So do natural materials of similar tone, such as unbleached linen and calico, and earthenware with a plain creamy glaze. Walls painted a neutral shade provide a gentler background than stronger colours for antique pieces hung on the walls – an old mirror, or textiles or rugs whose colours have become mellow with age. They work well too with contemporary works of art.

Eastern Light, Tusk, Heron, Mineral Gray, Glasgow Grey...these are some of the evocative names given to neutral and grey paints. Almost any handful can be used together happily – especially if they include paler and darker shades. Walls painted in neutrals complement the natural colour and patina of the finest hard-flooring materials, from milky marble to dusty slate in all its many varied shades, and the glorious warm depths of some much-polished terracotta tiles or bricks for flooring.

In a contemporary decorating scheme, one way to create variety and have a bit of fun with paint while retaining a sense of uncluttered spaciousness is to use exactly the same shade but in different finishes. Using matt and silk or gloss in the identical paint colour, you can make patterns on the walls, or even paint words, without being obvious. The pattern could be in the form of circles (larger and smaller, in lines or placed randomly), rings or stripes (horizontal or vertical). It could consist of frames around doors and windows, starbursts, lines of dots, or a personal or familiar motif. The larger and bolder the areas of different finish, the less work involved in preparation and fine-lining with a paintbrush (or application of low-tack masking tape).

You can use very slightly different tones of the same colour to achieve the same effect, one that will prompt people to look carefully and appreciate the humour of your decoration. This is the opposite to being knocked over by punchy bright colours.

Bright colour can, surprisingly, be an asset when you decorate a room predominantly in neutrals. A splash of strong colour gives focus to a room, and a single large item or a few items linked by colour will provide accents. In a room decorated in chalky whites and greys, a few bold items in purple or mauve, or blue or green, will bring the place to life without fighting the cool mood. In a room decorated in cream, a scarlet or burnt orange throw on a chair or bed, and a picture, lamp, vase or other object in a similar dominant colour, will give the room a lift. Accessories such as cushions and throws add a touch of spice and are easy to change with the seasons. Beware neutrals on their own becoming bland.

In one way, however, desert shades prevail over all other colours. The Modernists emphasized the plain flatness of their interior spaces with white paint, and similarly in contemporary decorating we can take inspiration from the neutral tones of modern construction materials. These are mostly very pale colours, shades of grey and neutrals: concrete, glass, bare plaster, blond wood, stainless steel, chrome, titanium (think of Frank O. Gehry & Associates' masterpiece, the Guggenheim Museum in Bilbao).

The contemporary aesthetic is to celebrate these materials, rather than to feel embarrassed by them or to try to cover them up (there is a parallel to this perhaps in attitudes to grey hair). We are glad to be twenty-first-century people in homes fit for our era. This does not mean, however, that we cannot cover up parts of the construction if we want to – a construction shell without any colour or comfort would be chilly indeed. A handmade rug on the floor will conceal a patch of floorboarding, but provides those other essential elements of contemporary decorating – luxury and texture – as well as offering an opportunity to introduce a block of delicious colour. A single wall (a tall, dramatic one, or a handsome curved one – something with interest) or a section of wall can be painted a rich, bright or pale but interesting colour for impact.

Painted wallcoverings now offer more than just colour and a degree of matt or gloss. The new generation of paints includes lustrous and metallic finishes, pearly sheen and even sparkle. Some of these are available as actual paints; some as washes that you add over your painted colour. You could also try making your own, adding aluminium powder to varnish or coloured paint – grey, in particular, will give you a metal-look finish. Metallic and pearly paints tend to be more expensive than other paint, but cost is relative and you will probably not want to paint an entire room with one of these delectable finishes. Choose a wall where the pearl or metallic will be displayed to best effect – a chimney breast, or a wall opposite a door or near a window where the light falling on it will enhance it.

There is also a huge choice of colourwashes offered by paint manufacturers in many tones, including the soft hues of desert and stone in all their shades of grey and creamy neutrals. These are 'clear' paints, with pigment added to allow you to add a glaze of one colour over another or to achieve a special effect such as stippling or sponging. One colour applied smoothly over another (especially if you use several coats of the wash) can give a depth to a painted wall that is appealing and really cannot be achieved in any other way, just as there is no short cut to the vibrant depth of genuine oriental lacquer.

Historically, neutrals were used to decorate hidden parts of nineteenth-century country houses, the corridors and service rooms inhabited by servants. These areas were painted pale colours because they were cheaply and easily obtained. Earlier, however, neutrals and pale shades were often used in grander rooms because their lightness accorded with the Georgian mood, and it was only the very rich who could afford the pigments for bright colours.

In the eighteenth and earlier nineteenth centuries, ages when there simply were not the paint colours whose brightness and availability we take for granted today, delicate differences in colour were considered seriously. Grey is a colour in point. There was dove grey, flaxen (possibly another term for 'French') grey, fine grey as opposed to inferior or ordinary grey, iron grey, mouse grey, light grey, silver grey, lead colour and slate grey. These were all made by taking white paint and adding touches of black and usually blue, as well as occasionally pink or red. Lavender was made with the same constituent colours, but the pink was added to the white first rather than last, with a little blue at the end. This shade was thought useful for ceilings in the nineteenth century because of its 'retiring appearance'.

The most famous of the cornucopia of grey paints was probably French grey, for which the addition of lake, rose pink or vermilion was essential to achieve its warmth and soft sophistication. The colour was called for in many grand houses in England, including Somerset House on the Thames in London and Great Saxham House in Suffolk, where Robert Adam specified it for the ceiling of the Oval Room. French grey is a colour one can imagine Jane Eyre and other heroines of nineteenth-century fiction wearing – not showy, but at the same time not unbecoming either.

Decorators used their own recipes for shades of colours, so they could also choose their own names (unlike a modern decorator ordering from a manufacturer). Thus, the tone used at Dyrham Park in Gloucestershire in 1781 was referred to, without apparent irony, as 'Dead French Gray'.

Of all the schools of decorating, historical and contemporary, the ones with which neutrals and greys are perhaps most closely identified today are the Japanese and the Swedish (or more specifically Gustavian) styles.

Traditional **Japanese homes** have walls constructed from white paper screens, floors covered with tatami mats made from pale woven grass, and mostly small, low pieces of furniture. There are cushions on the floor rather than sofas and chairs to sit on. This style has given inspiration to a generation of Western designers and decorators, who find its restraint elegant and uncluttered. The simple, pared-down look is an absolute necessity in Japan, where space is at a premium – most of the family's possessions are usually accommodated in a vast cupboard and only brought out when strictly needed. In the West we have more space, but the emptiness and pale colouring are appealing because they give our minds space in which to relax and roam. In small urban apartments, even in the West, Japanese style calls for an uncluttered existence.

Gustavian style was a chaste yet magical mixture of pale timber floors and plaster ceilings, with walls divided by a dado and painted in shades of grey and pastels. Rooms were furnished with elegant painted chairs and beds derived from French eighteenth-century designs. King Gustav, whose name is so familiar to us in connection with painted interior decoration, became ruler of Sweden in 1771.

Another significant date in Gustavian style was 1767, when a new design of stoves and heating pipes was invented that dramatically changed winter in that the better-off **Swedish homes**. Rich, sometimes deep, colours had previously been used on walls, but the paler, light-infused decorating schemes growing increasingly popular when Gustav III ascended the throne were now in tune with the liberation provided by the new heating systems, the focus of which was the **tiled stove**, so much more efficient (and potentially decorative) than an open fire.

Almost any one of a large number of Swedish manor houses of this period illustrate the typical elements of Gustavian style, among them the King's own castle of Gripsholm, where he had an extra wing of twenty-eight guest bedrooms built in about 1780.

In these bedrooms, the bottom portion of each wall is occupied by a tall skirting board (in reception and living rooms, this would be a panelled dado extending to the height of a chair), painted grey. Above this are pinned sheets of canvas, each the height of the room and painted to represent a white **panel decorated** with freehand **painted leaves**, flowers and, perched in a hoop suspended from a swag across the top, a single charming bird. Some rooms have a posy of flowers as the focus of each panel, with birds and butterflies darting about them.

Each panel is different and is completed by a pale grey surround. The doors and their frames are painted white; the scrubbed floorboards are pale (treated with lye and wax) and the furniture is painted too, in shades of cream and grey. The centrepiece of every room is the **stove**, covered with beautifully **decorated tiles**.

For a king to espouse such a restrained style so lacking in displays of pomp and gilding must say something about distinctively Swedish taste. Whatever the case, Gustavian style is not only uniquely appealing for its lightness and simplicity but also because it is easy to emulate. At the time, furniture was made from locally available pine, which was considered inferior to hardwoods and therefore disguised with paint. Today's softwood furniture can enjoy the same treatment which, more often than not, will improve its appearance.

Painting skirtings and doors in a tone such as grey can warm up a colour scheme that might otherwise be icily defined by the ubiquitous white gloss. **Grey-painted doors** in Gustavian interiors sometimes have panels picked out in white or another grey or pale shade, another device easily emulated. If they are not covered with lengths of fabric painted with panels of flowers and other **decorative motifs**, the walls above the dado are usually painted pastel shades, as in the charming top-floor rooms of the villa of Ekensberg on Lake Malaren. Here a light yellow on the walls is framed by pearly grey dado panelling and **architrave** around the window, and a **white cornice** and ceiling.

The Swedes were not the only people to rejoice in the restful-yet-varied quality offered by **tones of grey**. The poet William Wordsworth's home at Dove Cottage in the Lake District of England has timber wall panelling painted shades of grey. So does the drawing room at Hope Plantation, in North Carolina. The appeal of grey and the neutrals crosses ages and spaces to be as appealing again today, in our age of choice, as it was in generations when choice was so much more limited.

KALEIDO
SCOPE

'The first colours tha

impression on me we

white, carmine red, b

These memories go ba

of my life. I saw thes

objects which are no

mind as the colours t

made a strong

bright, juicy green,

ack and yellow ochre.

k to the third year

colours on various

onger as clear in my

emselves.'
W. Kandinsky, 1913

There is a fact about paint that makes it extraordinary. Think about it – no other decorating material is sold in a half-finished state. Only when we have bought it and put it on our wall (or floor, or ceiling or furniture), only when the solvent that constitutes about half the contents of the can has evaporated, only when the paint is dry do we see its real colour and finish.

But then, do we see it! Colour, brought to us by courtesy of paint, has arrived. The joy of colour, especially bright colour, is possible in our homes because modern paint is so easy to buy and apply. Scientists, technicians and manufacturers have worked to produce more convenient paint, each of many types fitted for a specific job, in a kaleidoscope of colours for our delight. Bright colour is life-enhancing. It lifts the spirit on a sunny day as well as a gloomy one. It is visual music for our eyes.

In this quick and slick world of ours, paint fulfils our need for change and excitement without causing too much actual disruption or costing the earth. A carnival of colours provides an antidote to historical carefulness – it is blatantly fun. It is sexy. We revel in the modernity of paint, and the colours it offers us. Vibrant purples, oranges, yellows, pinks, greens – these are colours and combinations of colours we have seen on the outside of Mexican buildings or caked on the faces of celebrants at Holi, colours that jingle-jangle at a fairground or circus, colours that leap out at us from product packaging designed to sell, sell, sell...

A kaleidoscope of colours appeals to us because it carries an element of risk. It represents freedom from convention – scarlet and saffron couldn't be further from the safe, fuddy-duddy colours we associate with institutions or public service buildings. Electric blue and violent violet romp around the house; fuschia and mango frolic. These colours are inviting. They sting the eye, they look juicy, they vibrate together, they are alive.

At the beginning of the twenty-first century, we are hungry for colour that reflects our status as contemporary beings. We crave colours that may be found in nature's exotic blooms and feathers, but which we more immediately associate with the fast-changing modern world and self-conscious artifice – bright packaging, advertising, hip-hop clothing, plastics, neon city lights, television. Some colours such as fluorescents may shock, some at the very least rip through our complacency to shout, 'Look at me'! Some are juxtaposed with others in combinations that are simply delightful, that make us smile. Multicolour fizzes in a way that rich historic colours cannot, beautiful as they are. Time and technology carry us forward on the crest of a wave of painted colour.

Our compulsion to be modern springs from the 1950s and '60s, when a post-war generation finally put behind itself the doom and gloom of the Second World War and rationing. The 1960s was the psychedelic age, when pattern went wild and so did colour. Combinations such as turquoise and emerald, as well as the ever-youthful black and white, could be seen on clothes as well as in homes. This was a time to be young with money to spend, and colourful graphic display was 'in'.

In the streets, colour spilled onto shop fronts. 'Flower power' meant that on the outside of such buildings as those in London's trendy Carnaby Street there was an eruption of colourful painted names and patterns. Colours overflowed and blended – red into pink into purple, yellow into orange. The look was hugely influential. In homes, the same effect could be seen on walls, where new wallpapers introduced bold and colourful printed pattern.

The 1970s continued the trend, and although this decade is now associated with the mustard/tan/olive school of colour scheme, there were actually gallons of bright colour about. Interiors created by the Danish designer Verner Panton demonstrate this, though at the time he was not well known internationally. In the late 1990s, Panton was 'discovered' by design museums, and through them and the media by a larger public that relished his puckish enthusiasm for life and colour. Typical Panton pronouncements include: 'I am not fond of white...there should be a tax on white paint', and 'To me colour is more important than form'.

Panton's Varna restaurant in Aarhus, designed in 1970, illustrated this. It had a purple carpet decorated with huge turquoise, royal and scarlet concentric circles. The ceiling was formed from bright blue, purple and orange globes the size of beach balls. Overall, the place was stunning in its use of colour. Panton designed whole interiors and also individual furniture and objects – his boldly curving plastic stacking chair has been hailed as a classic.

The 1980s were relatively subdued years in terms of colour, apart from the outburst of florid prints and flounces that erupted in the country house look. This was derived from a rediscovery of the charms of *le style anglais*, pioneered by Sybil Colefax. In the 1990s a different, pared-down aesthetic emerged.

Inspired by Japanese and oriental styles, and drawing on a reassessment of the Modernists and the work of such designers as the Eames in the 1950s, the 1990s revealed an attitude to decorating had been set free by modern technology. Efficient central heating (including the possibility of underfloor heating), pressurized hot water systems, double or triple glazing, sophisticated controls for all these and for lighting – such elements of domestic engineering have released us from the need to strive for a warm, comfortable environment. Instead of cover-up, the theme for the beginning of the new millennium was uncover. Let the building speak for itself.

Colour, and painted colour in particular, has an important role to play in contemporary decorating. You can choose to go wild with rampant pinks and reds, or use blues and greens in a restrained way to enliven a predominantly white or neutral scheme. It's up to you. Modern paint is inexpensive. You can buy it in almost any town, and if you can get to a bigger store you will find a dazzling choice of colours and finishes awaiting you. Take it home – it is easy to use, and should you make a mistake or have a better idea tomorrow it's no big deal. Change it! No need to feel embarrassed or extravagant. Go out and get another pot of paint.

Put your painted colour on one wall only (with a coat of white paint underneath to increase the brightness of bright colour). Or put it on a section of wall – behind a sofa or at the head of a bed to create a focus and give importance to that piece of furniture. Use different colours on different walls of a room (remembering that too many may create confusion). Or limit colour to squares or rectangles of colour, on canvases or painted directly onto the wall. A room can be transformed by bold use of clean painted colour. Enjoy the colour, but also enjoy the painted-ness of the colour. Celebrate paint.

You can use bright colour to create surprises. A room may look demure, painted and decorated in shades of grey and pale green, but open the door to walk through and bam! The shock of a bright green inner edge to the jamb hits you. When the door is closed, you can't see it; only when the door is opened is the narrow strip of bright colour revealed. Or paint the inside of your kitchen drawers and cupboards different bright colours – an exciting little secret you will enjoy every time you pull out a drawer. The inside of display cupboards can also benefit from painted colour to throw the contents into relief.

Colour can be used to manipulate space – to highlight the good points of a room and disguise less desirable ones. Bright colour in particular, because it tends to leap out at you, draws the eye to the part of a room where you want to focus attention or allow another element to go unnoticed. An example is a long, narrow room the far end of which you paint a bright colour, both to make it seem as wide as possible (you can also take the colour round on to neighbouring walls) and to draw it forward. An ugly fireplace that you don't want to remove can be 'hidden' by being painted the same colour as the wall.

Really interesting elements of a room can have attention drawn to them in this way. A curved wall could be painted a sumptuous shade to accentuate its sensual form. A window with an exceptional view can be 'dressed' with colour rather than with fabric curtains or blinds, leaving the maximum sight lines and letting in maximum daylight.

Use bright colour or combinations of colour on floors, too. A strongly coloured floor will draw attention to its full width. Paint the skirting board the same colour if you want the eye of the beholder to stretch the floor wider. A pattern of contrasts can be created with cork, MDF or hardboard tiles, painted two or more different colours before being laid in a random or chequerboard pattern.

Painted colour can be used to create enclosure, and to provoke movement. Lead the eye from one space into another by painting the further room or passage a colour that grabs you with its brightness, or use a colour that is significant but subsidiary in the first room. Or use a complementary colour – red with green, for example, or yellow with purple – to create a frisson. Complementaries are the colours opposite each other on the colour 'wheel', created by placing the primaries (red, yellow and blue) at equal intervals around a circle and filling in the gaps with all the degrees of combination of the neighbouring primaries.

One of the aspects of contemporary decorating that people find hardest is combining colours. Some obviously go together – blue and white, for example. But mixing colours other than white or shades of the same colour can cause a headache. Fortunately, there is a wealth of visual material to help you discover colour combinations you like, and that work together. The important thing is to relax when you use colour – don't agonize or worry about good taste.

The first place to look is in your own home. Are there coloured objects that you like, especially any you want to use in the room for which you are seeking inspiration? Do these colours work together? What about any product packaging you have around the house? Expert designers spend large quantities of their clients' money devising seductive colour combinations, so you may be able to pick up some clues from their work for free. Even the spines of the books on your shelves can offer suggestions.

Other home-grown ideas can be found in your wardrobe. The fashion world regularly gives the lead to the world of interiors in choices of texture and colour. Your clothes presumably include colours that you like. Also look at the landscape around your home, be it in the country or the city. Look at buildings, foliage and flowers for colour combinations.

One of the guidelines of classic decorating is that you choose patterns first when decorating a room, then add the flat colour later. This may not apply to contemporary decorating, but you can still look to textiles for ideas for colour combinations. Curtain fabrics, cushions, lampshades, woven or printed textiles, embroidery...any of these can show you how colours work together. So can artefacts – pots, jewellery, leatherwork.

Look at things you like, in your own home, in other people's and elsewhere, and notice how colour is used to decorate them. Make notes – mental, written and visual (in the form of cuttings, colour cards, scraps of fabric, sweet wrappers, postcards of art, anything with colour) – of combinations you don't like as well as ones you do, to help you develop your taste and an 'eye' for colour.

Travel and the natural world across the globe is another fabulous source of inspiration. The distinctive electric multicolouring of houses in Mexico, typified in the buildings of Luis Barragán were, ironically, influenced by Moroccan and Islamic styles of architecture and decoration. His hot, romantic use of colour is a million miles from the tonal restraint of the European modernists, as well as being on the other side of the world. When travelling, look at the colours of the buildings and costumes, flora and fauna, landscape and seascape of other countries, and the combinations of colours you find there, often wonderfully different from those at home. Celebrate that difference. Take snapshots when you're away and scour the travel press for images to feed the eye and the imagination. Keep a pinboard on which to secure your collection of images so that you can think about colour every day.

Art offers yet another rich treasure trove of colour sources. Artists, after all, have an innate sense of design that has been nurtured by training and experience. Look at the work of the great colourists, from Henri Matisse through Mark Rothko to Patrick Heron and Bridget Riley. Each of these artists uses striking or bright colour to create drama. They also use combinations of bright colour in ways that are endlessly exhilarating. But if looking at art seems intimidating, don't panic! Simply try out a colour combination that you have seen in someone else's home, in a book such as this one or in a magazine.

It is difficult to say how large an expanse of painted colour you need to create an effect, or whether you can have too much colour. So much depends on the individual room, what is to go into it in the way of furniture and furnishings, the look of your home as a whole, and the way that you see through from space to space. Much also depends on your taste. Trust your own instinct. Only be wary of too much of the same bright colour.

The only real way to find out how much colour to use is to plunge in. You can either start with white and gradually **build up colour**, painting walls or parts of walls until you find that your delight tells you that you have reached your own point of saturation. This is perhaps the easiest way to discover your colour limits. Or you can splash out, painting large areas and, if you find you have been too extravagant and the colours are too noisy, simply delete them. All it takes to get the balance right is a relaxed, open mind and the time to make decisions and act on them.

One of the joys of modern paints is the way they can be used to create various transformations. There is a **primer** and/or paint that will cling to almost every conceivable surface, giving you the opportunity to change its colour without the upheaval and cost of removing and replacing it. The latest can withstand the wear and tear that would have reduced the best product of a few years ago to a scratched and tatty mess. The cost of such transformations often drops after a product has lost its initial novelty and spawned competitors.

Primers are available to prepare the surfaces of melamine and metal for painted colour. For metal, there is the popular alternative of car spray paint, designed to be glossy, tough and good-looking. So-called 'white' goods such as refrigerators and dishwashers are available in other colours now, but usually only at the top end of the market and even then only at a price. How much simpler to unite them with the colours in the rest of your kitchen by rubbing them down with sandpaper, first coarse then fine, before painting the same colour.

Radiators can quickly and easily be transformed, and with no need for expensive or specialist paint. Ordinary **emulsion** will do the job and enable you to hide the radiator by painting it exactly the same colour as the wall. Make sure that the radiator is clean before you start, sand it lightly to give the paint a 'key' then clean off the dust with a tack rag or very slightly damp cloth. The radiator should be dry and completely cold when you paint it and until the paint is entirely dry.

Even **kitchen** work surfaces can be painted – a godsend when the alternative is a costly refit. A suitable primer for the job is one that actually forms a bond with the impervious surface of the plastic coating. Usually this takes an hour or two to dry, and a week or more to cure completely. Paint, or a product such as Illumitex, can be applied once the primer is dry. Illumitex is a 'paint' system that sprays any **surface** (walls, floor or even ceiling, as well as countertops and furniture) with a shimmer of metallic-look PVA particles. You seal this with the hardest varnish available. Don't place anything on the surface until after the primer has cured as any pressure will leave indentations.

New paint products and novel systems like Illumitex are constantly being introduced by manufacturers and retailers. If you live near a decorators' centre rather than just a DIY store, you may find it worth a regular visit. People who sell a product in which they are genuinely interested are usually happy to talk about it. Many specialist shops test products themselves so that they can talk about them from experience, and this also enables them to recommend one product over another for a particular task.

Paint is an ever-changing medium. Our interest in its possibilities extends in many directions. We are fascinated by its immediate decorative possibilities and by the expanding field of understanding the science, techniques and decorative use of paint in previous decades and centuries. Not least, we are excited to know what is yet to come. Manufacturers are also interested – paint is their market and they need to keep ahead.

There are many ways forward for paint in the new millennium, many of them no doubt as yet unfathomable, beyond our imagination. Some, however, can be guessed at, and some of the newest ideas are also entertaining to contemplate. Scented paint is one. This is already available for children, in delicious water-melon 'flavour' for example. The scent fades away, however. Currently, it is designed to make paint fun for the child while it is being applied and to mask the smell.

Paints also need to become cleaner, kinder, less polluting. Governments in the developed world are already pressing for this with rules and regulations that promote the phasing out of toxic substances. With our children in mind, we need to support them in this. Some pigments, such as those based on lead, mercury or arsenic, cannot be used today for health and safety reasons, as they are injurious both to the manufacturers and the consumers. Real cochineal, made from the crushed bodies of South American beetles, is no longer used, and neither are vegetable dyes. The colours these would have provided are not lost but simply replaced by safe organic chemical substitutes.

There is continuing interest in paints for special effects that simulate, for example, patchy old plaster, fresco painting or limewash. The limit on these, from the general manufacturer's point of view is that they must be ready to use and foolproof. These requirements present problems. Specialist outlets sell their own kits, and decorators who are expert in this field demonstrate unusual effects in books and magazines and on television.

Paint effects are as much a craft or hobby in this context. The simplest paint effect is probably **colourwash**, which involves applying a tinted glaze (a clear paint, without opacity) over a plain painted wall (see the *Ideas in Practice* section).

In the future, you may be able to control the exact degree of **gloss or shine** in your chosen paint. Another possible advance in paint science would be the development or discovery of a pigment with the same superb opacity as titanium dioxide, but which has the opposite quality of absorbing rather than reflecting light. Some earth pigments such as red oxide have good opacity and are used in dark colours, and lead chrome pigments are impressively opaque too, but their use in domestic paints is prohibited. It is the carnival colours (saturated bright yellow, red, orange and blue) that would benefit, as these have inferior opacity today.

Digital manipulation of colour may well be possible in the home, however, as it is in advertising and photography, by using computer technology. It is already perfectly possible to alter the colour of your room using light. Paint the walls white and use hidden bulbs to wash them with shades of blue, yellow or pink at the setting of a switch, the colour you choose depending on your mood, the weather and the seasons. Effects such as iridescence and strobe are now possible, with the inclusion in the paint of tiny particles that affect the way **light** plays upon them.

In contrast to today's demand for quick, dramatic results, looking to the past for inspiration has a large and growing following. Hence the success of 'historic' paints. Certain paint manufacturers are increasingly making paints available that would have been familiar to our great-grandparents. In this they are supported by their customers, by organizations of interested people, and by the institutional and private owners of **historic buildings**.

There is perhaps a lesson to be learned from this attitude of bringing the best of the past forward, even if we are using modern paints. We may learn not to treat paint as a convenience product, or not *only* to treat it as such. If we devote greater time to achieving **depth of colour** – with many more coats, for example – or to daring to experiment with a wider variety of types of paint, we will reap the rewards.

To end on a note that faces the past and the future, **colour, texture** and **finish** are the three pivots of contemporary attitudes to decorating, which appeal to us on a sensual, emotional level as well as on a practical one. **Paint** is a medium for colour with superb qualities that we must celebrate, to set colour free in our homes and our lives.

IDEAS IN
PRACTICE

Some of the techniques that appear elsewhere in this book are explored in this section in greater detail. *Paint: The Fired Earth Book of Natural Colour* is not a do-it-yourself manual and so *Ideas in Practice* is not intended to be a comprehensive guide. Its purpose is to expand on some interesting points mentioned in previous chapters.

DISTEMPER

The traditional forerunner of emulsion, this gives a warm soft finish, rather like whitewash or limewash. It is supplied ready mixed or as a creamy paste that needs thinning with water. As distemper allows the walls to breathe, it is suitable for old buildings that are prone to damp.

LACQUER

Traditional Chinese lacquer paints require many coats to build up the depth of colour that can now be achieved with just two or three coats of the more durable and glossy modern equivalent.

LIMEWASH

The history and use of this wonderful paint is described in Chapter one, *Arctic Tints*. Limewash is much more than a historic paint, however. Although we have got out of practice, it is perfectly possible to make and use it today. It is, in fact, a wonderfully simple concoction with only two necessary ingredients: quicklime and water. An understanding of the process is perhaps the other pre-requisite, in terms of both safety and of your enjoyment of the experience.

The basic material is quicklime (calcium oxide, a product of burning chalk and limestones), which looks like white powdery pebbles in the sack. It can be obtained from specialist suppliers. The quicklime is then 'slaked', which simply means mixing it carefully into some water in a bucket (or, traditionally, a pit dug in the ground). When you add the quicklime to the water and stir it, breaking up the lumps, a chemical reaction takes place. This results in the mixture becoming fizzing hot. It steams, bubbles and hisses dramatically. Once the slaking is complete

and the mixture has calmed, you add more water until sloppy, then strain it.

It is possible to buy already slaked lime in a paste form, which you dilute at home, and you can even obtain readymade limewash fairly easily. This is a convenient and safe route to take if you want the finished result of limewash, but it is more impersonal and lacking in the immediacy, satisfaction and sensual power that comes from making your own.

Before you start working with lime, take the precaution of wearing sensible clothes, with your arms and legs covered. You should wear sturdy gloves and goggles to protect your eyes, just in case. Another preparatory step is to ensure that the wall you plan to paint is brushed down, with no loose bits of old limewash or flakes of stone or brick.

So that the mixture doesn't splash, paint on the limewash with a short-bristled brush. If you want an even finish rather than a rustic patchy one, slosh water on to the wall before applying the limewash to reduce its absorbency differentials. The irregular finish has its own attractions, however. In the market for modern paints and 'paint effects', specialists and decorators make great efforts to reproduce exactly this rustic impression.

One of the mistakes frequently made with limewash is to make it too thick. In the bucket, limewash of the correct, runny consistency looks transparent and thin. In fact, it becomes opaque as it dries, and several thin coats are better than a few thicker ones. In the right conditions (well-ventilated, not too humid or too cold) limewash dries quickly and can be re-coated in a few hours.

Wonderful though it is, there are a few limitations to the use of limewash. It works by soaking into the surface of a porous material, so it cannot be used over existing modern paints which are, by their nature, not porous. Use it only over bare stone, brick, plaster or previous layers of limewash or distemper (rubbed

down first). Modern plaster skim is also too smooth and shiny to absorb limewash effectively, but modern bonding plaster, which is grittier and coarser and is used underneath the skim, usually accepts it. Wood also presents problems. Although it is porous, it is also flexible while finished limewash is not. Limewash can, however, be painted onto exterior (and interior) new construction timber, then wiped off as it dries, to even out the appearance of differences in colour before the timber weathers or seasons.

COLOURED LIME PAINT

Limewash, in spite of also being known as whitewash, does not always have to be white. Coloured pigment can be added to the ready limewash (if you are using powder, mix it with water first), remembering that the dry paint on the wall will be considerably lighter than the colour you mix in the bucket. Traditionally, a twist of blue pigment was often added at the last minute to brighten the white – the same pigment (still known in parts of the North of England as 'dolly blue') that laundresses added to the washing water accentuate the whiteness of garments.

Powdered pigments are available from specialist outlets (which frequently offer a mail order service). They give you the opportunity to experiment with colour, mixing your own into the limewash until you are happy.

MASONRY PAINT

Masonry paint protects and decorates exteriors. Use it on concrete, exterior brickwork, stone, rough-cast rendering and pebbledash. It is durable and contains fungicide to inhibit mould.

PAINT EFFECTS

The idea of using paint on the walls of our homes for special effect rather than as areas of flat colour has a long history, starting with the cavemen. Today's murals take this idea to an extreme, but there are many other effects that can be used in an entire room. These have come a long way since the 1970s and '80s, and rag-rolling and sponging seem clumsy and obvious to us now. Contemporary special effects are more subtle. Some, such as stencilling, colourwashing and dragging have peasant origins and can still be seen on buildings in the South of France and farmhouses in Italy and New England. Other effects listed are more modern and sophisticated.

CONTRAST PATTERNS

The subtlest of paint effects is achieved without any change in colour at all. Use

the same colour but in two contrasting finishes – matt and glossy, for example – and paint patterns on the wall with them. The patterns could be in the form of wide horizontal bands stretching around the room, concentric circles, squares within squares or a frieze of shapes around the top of the room.

VARNISHING

This is similar to the above technique, but uses varnish instead of gloss paint. The varnished areas will have a subtly different colour as well as added sheen. This effect is especially splendid over metallic paints, giving the varnished areas a depth and richness akin to Asian or oriental lacquer.

DENIM

This comes as a special kit, or you can employ a professional decorator to do it for you as it involves several layers of paint and varnish. It also requires a steady hand to produce the long streaks that are, effectively, dragging carried smoothly and evenly to the full height of the room from floor to ceiling. A variation is the full fabric effect. This involves painting a base colour on to the wall before dragging two layers with a fine comb or wire wool, one vertically then, when that is dry, the other horizontally. For the denim effect, the top layer is a darker tone of the

bottom coat; for the fabric effect, choose a paler base coat than the colour of the 'fabric', with both top layers the same colour as each other and slightly darker than the base. You can also mix the colour for the top coats with some glaze for a silky effect.

CRAQUELURE

Another special paint finish, which has been popular ever since the eighteenth-century vogue for oriental decorative objects, is craquelure. This is a network of tiny cracks in paintwork that gives the impression of antiquity. It can be reproduced on any smooth, flat (in the sense of being without mouldings – a curved lamp or jar is fine), rigid surface. The technique is often used on objects such as lamps, boxes, trays and so on, but it can also be used on entire walls, to dramatic effect. Two layers of paint are separated by a layer of crackle glaze that will split and crack the top layer, revealing the colour of the base coat. The two coats of paint can be the same colour, different shades of the same colour, or different colours.

PAINTING WOOD

It is well worth taking some time and trouble to prepare wood thoroughly for painting. If they have been in place for some time, you may want to refresh the form of mouldings and architrave by stripping them of old paint that is clogging up the grooves. Any existing paint on a surface that you are not going to strip should be clean and free of flakes and loose pieces. Sand the surface lightly to provide grip for the new paint, finishing off with a tack rag or slightly damp cloth to lift the sanding dust.

Knots in new timber need to be sealed with 'knotting' (a shellac-based product) to prevent these flaws weeping a resinous substance that could cause blotches on the finished paint surface. An alternative, if you intend using a translucent stain or a paint in a liming effect, is to seal new knots with a little white wax polish. This will not show through in the same way as knotting, which is brown.

STAMPING PATTERN

Stamping has a long history, both on textiles and on painted wall decoration. The process is quite simple. You use a flat stamp, today made of photopolymer, a slightly rubbery plastic. You coat this with paint, using a roller that you have primed in a tray or dish of paint, then you press the stamp against the wall where you want the imprint to appear. It is a similar technique to making wood-cut or lino-cut prints, or printing with a cut-out sponge.

The great practical advantage that stamping has over the other traditional technique of stencilling is in the designs it is possible to reproduce by this method. A stamped pattern can have 'floating' parts, not attached to any other part. Stencils, however, are cut out of a sheet and all parts of the pattern have therefore to be firmly attached to others, or they simply drop off (imagine cutting a pattern out of a piece of paper).

The latest designs of bought-in stamp include funky geometric shapes such as rectangles within rectangles, and circles within circles, which you can use repeated alone or in combination with each other. Some suppliers will also make a custom stamp to your own design, which could include your initials or other personal motif. Or you could make a simple stamp from a lino-cut (with a timber offcut glued to the back to make a handle) or halved potato (first test its performance with your paint).

WOODGRAINING

It is perfectly possible to create your own woodgraining, marbling or even tortoise-shell effects using modern paints available from a craft or art shop or specialist supplier, and with the help of a DIY decorating manual. You may indeed gain considerable satisfaction from having 'done it myself', especially if you do not dissipate your energies in bemoaning the fact that your efforts are not perfect – neither is the grain of any wood, and no one else will be as critical of your efforts as you are yourself.

FIRED EARTH
Head Office, Warehouse
and Factory Shop
Twyford Mill, Oxford Rd
Adderbury
BANBURY Oxfordshire
OX17 3HP, UK
Tel: 01295 812088
Fax: 01295 810832
Email and website:
enquiries@firedearth.com
export@firedearth.com
www.firedearth.com

**FIRED EARTH
LONDON
SHOWROOMS**
174 Chiswick High Road
CHISWICK, W4 1PR
Tel: 020 8994 5355/4353

117–119 Fulham Road
SW3 6RL
Tel: 020 7589 0489

41 Heath Street
HAMPSTEAD, NW3 6UA
Tel: 020 7435 1473

102 Portland Road
W11 4LX
Tel: 020 7221 4825

58 High Street
WIMBLEDON, SW19 5EE
Tel: 020 8879 0855

BATHROOM SHOWROOM
229 Ebury Street
SW1W 8UT
Tel: 020 7823 4549

AROUND UK
3 Saracen Street
BATH
Avon BA1 5BR
Tel: 01225 442594

23 Bruce Street
BELFAST BT2 7JD
Tel: 02890 238000

10–12 North Bar Within
BEVERLEY
East Yorkshire HU17 8AX
Tel: 01482 864878

63 Poole Road
Westbourne
BOURNEMOUTH
BH4 9BA
Tel: 01202 766441

15C Prince Albert Street
BRIGHTON BN1 1HF
Tel: 01273 719977

65A Whiteladies Road
(on Aberdeen Road)
Clifton
BRISTOL BS8 2LY
Tel: 0117 973 7400

3 Bridge Street
CAMBRIDGE CB2 1UA
Tel: 01223 300941

15A Burgate
CANTERBURY CT1 2HG
Tel: 01227 764944

57 Moulsham Street
CHELMSFORD
Essex CM2 0JA
Tel: 01245 494684

25 Clarence Parade
CHELTENHAM
Gloucestershire
GL50 3PA
Tel: 01242 251455

36 Lower Bridge Street
CHESTER
Cheshire CH1 1RS
Tel: 01244 348084

13A Eastgate Square
CHICHESTER
W. Sussex PO19 1JL
Tel: 01243 538523

101 High Street
COLCHESTER
Essex CO1 1TH
Tel: 01206 543525

29 Castle Street
EDINBURGH EH2 3DN
Tel: 0131 220 2611

83 St Vincent Street
GLASGOW G2 5TF
Tel: 0141 204 0917

2 Chapel Street
GUILDFORD
Surrey GU1 3UH
Tel: 01483 300052

4–6 Cheltenham Parade
HARROGATE HG1 1DB
Tel: 01423 529991

43 Eign Gate
HEREFORD HR4 0AB
Tel: 01432 277000

1 High Street
HUNGERFORD
Berkshire RG17 0DN
Tel: 01488 680707

36 Market Place
KINGSTON UPON
THAMES
Surrey KT1 1JQ
Tel: 020 8549 6655

5–9 Sir Simons Arcade
(off Market Street)
LANCASTER LA1 1JL
Tel: 01524 841020

114 Regent Street
LEAMINGTON SPA
Warwickshire CV32 4NR
Tel: 01926 886125

80 Vicar Lane
LEEDS LS1 7JH
Tel: 0113 2448404

Vale Farm
Woburn Road
LIDLINGTON
Bedfordshire MK43 0NL
Tel: 01234 765765

78 Bishops Centre,
Taplow, MAIDENHEAD
Berkshire SL6 0NY
Tel: 01628 661900

16 John Dalton Street
MANCHESTER M2 6HY
Tel: 0161 8323122

44 Mosley Street
NEWCASTLE UPON TYNE
NE1 1DF
Tel: 0191 221 2661

Applegarth Building
220A High Street
NORTHALLERTON
North Yorkshire DL7 8LU
Tel: 01609 774402

7 St Giles Street
NORWICH NR2 1JL
Tel: 01603 619612

14 King Street
NOTTINGHAM
Nottinghamshire
NG1 2AY
Tel: 0115 947 6534

Hewits Farm
Court Road, Chelsfield
ORPINGTON
Kent BR6 7RQ
Tel: 01959 534824

13 Woodstock Road
OXFORD
Oxon OX2 6HA
Tel: 01865 514549

21 Winchester Street
SALISBURY
Wiltshire SP1 1HB
Tel: 01722 414554

South Street
SHERBORNE DT9 3TD
Tel: 01935 817900

42 High Street
SHREWSBURY SY1 1ST
Tel: 01743 344155

38 Poplar Road
SOLIHULL
West Midlands B91 3AB
Tel: 0121 704 3605

60 Holywell Hill
ST ALBANS
Hertfordshire AL1 1BX
Tel: 01727 855407

76 Calverley Road
TUNBRIDGE WELLS
Kent TN1 2UY
Tel: 01892 540220

2 Church Street
WILMSLOW
Cheshire SK9 1AU
Tel: 01625 548048

OUTSIDE UK
Nikolaj Plads 11
1067 COPENHAGEN
DENMARK
Tel: 3393 9331

Koenigstrasse 5
30175 HANNOVER
GERMANY
Tel: 0511 3360508

2404 Dominion Centre
43–59 Queens Road East
WANCHAI, HONG KONG
Tel: 286 13864

31 Lower Ormonde Quay
DUBLIN, IRELAND
Tel: 01283 3880

SDN BHD
Lot 6–0 Ground Floor
Lintas Plaza
Lrglintas Plaza 3
Luyang 8830
Kota Kinabalu
SABAH, MALAYSIA
Tel: 088 245159

Brickhouse BV
Stieltjesstraat 116
3071 JX ROTTERDAM
THE NETHERLANDS
Tel: 010 290 7050

Bygdoy Alle 56
0265 OSLO, NORWAY
Tel: 2243 6270

Chalmersgatan 21
S 41135 GOTHENBURG
SWEDEN
Tel: 3116 7520

Nybrogatan 3
S 11434 STOCKHOLM
SWEDEN
Tel: 8611 8117

INTRODUCTION

The startling white face of the barn owl (*Tyto alba*) reveals its keen black eyes and feathers that are arranged with astonishing precision.

A stunning impact is achieved here by simply dabbing irregular spots of black paint on white. While modern in spirit, this is in fact an interior from the Peter Wentz Farmstead in the United States, which was decorated in 1744 by German Menonite settlers.

The pale, softened splendour of ancient stone carvings in Israel, with their worn down leaves harbouring sand in the curves and crevices.

A regular pattern of lines of neat spots on the wall, each column diminishing and then increasing in size, is reminiscent of the Pop Art of Bridget Riley and others in the 1960s. The white floor and ceiling emphasize the design by Leo Santos-Shaw. Cushions in vibrant colours extend the geometric theme.

Frost, sharp and fresh, shows up each separate twig and leaf on winter trees, throwing into relief the texture of bark.

Anne Rueyeres has decorated the walls of her apartment in Marseilles in the South of France using a form of limewash coloured with ochre earth pigments and with sand added for a rougher texture. She so liked the trial patches of colour that she left them.

Under the microscope, the hairs of polar bears' fur has been shown to be transparent – the colour we see is a reflection, literally, of their environment. These bears are playing in the snow of Manitoba, Canada.

The shape and colour of old lichen-streaked terracotta garden pots is a familiar and reassuring sight, whether or not they have plants in them.

White is not simply one colour – it is a family of shades approximating to our idea of white. Here on Tahiti, the dresses, hats and gloves of worshippers at the Temple di Papeete offer a range of tones varying from milk to cream.

Wonderful spots and dots in raving colours, on *Small Circles Painting* (1996) by Peter Davies, seem to have a vibrant life of their own as they dance across the canvas.

The chalky white cliffs of Dover, on the south coast of England, constantly renew themselves with landslips. The nearest paint effect for recreating their soft, matt whiteness is achievable by (making and) using consecutive coats of watery limewash.

The breathtaking view of patterned clouds against blue skies – their colour tones, mood and atmosphere – never cease to amaze.

Set against soft old terracotta tiles and the noble chestnut beams of an old Spanish house, a white-painted wall and white linen sofa cover seem soft and mellow on account of their matt finish and tactile surfaces.

ARCTIC TINTS

The Georgian home of textile entrepreneur Lena Proudlock is painted white, lifted with a touch of gold leaf on the raised mouldings of the cupboard doors, all of which are reminiscent of the Gustavian elegance of her parents' home in Sweden.

The newly revealed layers from peeling bark on this silver birch tree are virgin white; over time the surface will weather to become papery shades of mushroom, sand and soil, as have the aged layers on top.

A sophisticated all-white interior can be difficult to maintain, but it's the ultimate in purity and lack of compromise. White flowing covers and some dark wood antique furniture soften the impact of white paint and lessen its iciness in the home of Alexander Vethers, an Austrian artist based in New York City.

Architect Claudio Silvestrin has created the ultimate serene interior in this riverside apartment, balancing white with the warm tones of natural wood, and keeping shapes plain and geometric.

This is not a sea anemone but the flowerhead of the gardener's friend, a hardy *Echinops ritro*, the globe thistle, which thrives best in full sun and poor soil.

OCEAN WASH

A large blue-painted vintage car makes an outstanding impact against a shabby brown wall, its colour providing a visual link with the bright Cuban sky beyond.

This breathtaking scene shows chinstrap penguins on an extraordinary formation created by ancient compressed ice. This rare blue iceberg is in Antarctica.

This intensely-painted blue building in India draws us in, making us long to explore the recesses of archway and staircase which dazzle the eye.

From far above, a helicopter looks like a spec, perhaps a small bird, against the intense greeny-blue ocean wash on the Hardy Reef off Queensland, Australia.

Blue water-based paint applied roughly over a solid white undercoat gives the impression of a few wispy white clouds in a seamless cerulean sky. An idyllic scene on the Greek island of Santorini.

The blue-and-white cross of St Andrew, Scotland's patron saint, is transformed into war paint by rugby world cup fans at the Scotland vs. Uruguay match at Murrayfield, Edinburgh.

Peasant homes around the Mediterranean (this is on the island of Ibiza) habitually had a broad band of bright painted colour along the bottom of the walls and around window openings to disguise the marks of wear, a tradition which can be used to decorative effect today.

The amazing blue feet of a Blue-footed Booby (*Sula nebouxi*) look unreal and abstract, seen close-up here on a rock on the Galapagos Islands.

The seaside appeal of walls painted Wedgwood blue with fresh white woodwork can be used anywhere, in town or country, to create a cool open-air feeling. Snowy white towels and a bright blue laundry bag accentuate the look.

How reminiscent of pastoral summers in temperate climes are the delicate flowers called Love-in-a-mist (*Nigella damascena*).

This might once have been a dull little back hall – no longer! By marking off the entire space, walls, doors and woodwork into squares and painting a chequer-board of blue and white (probably all-white first, the blue applied afterwards), designer James Merifield has transformed his home.

Is this a school outing, or one man's extensive family? Eight young children are protected from the rain by identical blue nylon hooded capes in Hue, Vietnam.

A deep, indigo blue on the surface of the units and splashback in the kitchen of bakery owner Gail Stephens gives the room a serious serenity.

The limpid beauty of this little reptile belies its nature – it is a Poison Arrow frog (*Dendrobates azureus*) – as it sits demurely on a tropical leaf.

Not only is this a deliciously glossy, blue room with shiny floor and matt walls, it is also a new concept in abluting. Designer Diego Fortunata designed the 'Acqua' chaise longue for Perobell and installed one in his own bathroom, which he conceived as a public and social space for friends or family.

Colour applied with paint has been used as a unifying element in this charming French kitchen. Walls, shelves, units and dishwasher have been painted the same delicate shade. To achieve this, scour the surface of white goods with rough sandpaper and wipe with a tacky cloth before applying a suitable paint.

Our attention is drawn to this sensuously curving wall in a seaside barn conversion in north Norfolk, England, by the lustrous sea-green colour painted onto it. The architect of this project was Chris Cowper.

Today, everybody needs a home office. This one, by designer Jonty Henshall, is very different to an ordinary filing cabinet. Clad in rough-sawn timber that has been washed with household emulsion, it has driftwood pieces for handles, sanded to remove the splinters.

A cool, soft green seems almost to dissolve before the eye in the heat, in this kitchen at the holiday home of Pepe Lagos in Punta del Este, Uruguay.

FOREST HUES

Looking from the salon through to the veranda that overhangs the interior courtyard garden of a house on the Canary Islands, our eye is caught by the painted lattice screen or *jalousie*.

This cheerful cheesemaker from Sussex, England, is holding a classic cheddar in his hands. The bright solid green of his apron makes an astringent contrast to the faded, distressed paintwork on the door behind him.

Evocatively named 'Africa', this farmhouse built in about 1846 in New York State is as bright in winter as in summer. Designer Frank Benedict, inspired by eighteenth-century colour schemes, has used clean, strong tones like the fresh leaf green in the drawing room beyond.

A rosette of sword-shaped leaves makes *Agave parryi* one of the most architectural small succulents. Its glaucous grey-blue tone is restful on the eye.

Palest pale green, like the colour of a Chinese vase, colours the walls of photographer David Seidner's atelier in the fifteenth-century Arrondissement of Paris, giving it an air of utter restraint.

Just the sight of water droplets, making a reptilian pattern on blades of luscious green grass, makes one thirsty.

Certain mid-range greens have the ability to be both vibrant and restful, classic and contemporary, at different times of the day and night depending on the quality of daylight and your mood. The neutral tones of a metal table and the bare unfinished plank floor are the perfect foil.

Over the years, moss has softened and greened the surfaces of monumental stone carvings at Ubud, Bali, Indonesia.

Rather than the walls, it is the furniture in this Parisian home that is painted with colour – green chairs and grey table are antiques and probably with their original distressed paintwork. China on display is a collection of Wedgwood and Creil.

Like discarded beads flung aside by an ancient Greek goddess, these sea urchins' carapaces pile up on Alonissos Island.

EARTH TONES

A mosaic of green tiles, highlighted with blue, white and reddish-brown, in the King Hassan II mosque, Morocco.

The brilliant red of this autumnal oak leaf will burn itself out in a day or two, turning brown like all the others on the twig.

Shells of nuts – walnuts, Brazil nuts, peanuts and hazelnuts – each a different shape, texture and shade of brown, each hold its brittle treasure within.

Patricia de las Carreras has renovated the paintwork of her nineteenth-century home in Buenos Aires, picking out the bold zig-zag of the stairs' risers and treads in white. The edge of any architectural feature can be given this treatment for a contemporary, graphic look.

How astonishing is a close-up view of the skin of the reticulated giraffe (*Giraffa camelopardalis reticulata*) and how similar it is to the cracked earth pattern.

The fabulous interior of the museum at Delsbro, Skansen, displays a variety of Swedish folk art, including splatter paint on the dado, decorative patterns in rooms beyond and, on the near wall, an original technique of traditional wall painting.

The surface of red, sun-baked soil has finally succumbed to dry heat here, making it split open like the flaking husk of a nut.

A bathroom in a small house among the Burgundy vineyards has been given added interest by painting the existing tiles in various shades of cream, red, grey and brown. Paint on the wooden door has been left in its distressed state.

Hot toast, about to be buttered, has an inviting golden-brown mottled surface with slightly charred stripes. It speaks to us of fireside teas, winter afternoons and the warmth of home.

The bedroom of Tatyana Hill's home in north London is painted a ravishing milk-chocolate brown, good enough to eat. Elsewhere, bookshelves are painted the same colour but brushed over with silver leaf, and feathers decorate the top edges of the walls.

In an ancient, academic library the spines of leather-bound books have a soothing rhythm. Their tones of brown have an organic quality that moulds with the wood of shelves and ladder so that they all seem part of one whole.

DESERT SHADES

Few can resist the luxury of dark, bitter chocolate cake, drawing us in with its indescribable scent, its velvety texture and rich flavour, to create an air of utter seduction.

Storm clouds rage over a desert landscape. The photographer has captured the exact moment when lightning has split the sky above the rain that thunders down onto the sands.

A healthy hen – you can tell by the glossiness of her scarlet comb and russet feathers, and the brightness of her eye – nestles in the tweed-clad crook of a farmer's arm.

Giorgio Morandi (1890–1964) was an Italian painter who lived his entire life in the town of Bologna, his birthplace. The poetic quality of his still lifes, executed in a narrow range of tones like the subtle greys and browns seen here, won him many admirers. This *Still Life with Bottles* was painted the year before he died.

A husband-and-wife team built this house (him) in materials authentic to the area of Oostzaan, Holland, and decorated it (her) in a warm, bold, contemporary style. Chalky matt paint on the walls is a dry, pebbly shade.

The outraged expression of this gargoyle at Blois, Loire-et-Cher in France, is forever frozen in the grey stone from which he was carved, now softened by a growth of dry mottled lichen.

The fireplace on the patio of a house in Marrakech has been cleverly painted in three earthy colours to accentuate the layers of its construction.

The beautiful cat that is the Siberian lynx (*Lynx l. wrangeli*) has yellow eyes and fur whose mottled tones allow it to fade into the landscape as it stalks its prey.

The moon is not made of cheese, it is made of rock and dust, as we can see in this astonishing photograph of our planet's faithful satellite.

The glamour of this bathroom, with its cool and sophisticated grey, white and silver theme, belies its location in a cottage in Surrey, England, albeit a large and spacious one.

Thousands of years of grinding on sea shores turns pebbles to sand; in the meantime their softened, rounded edges and many-coloured hues make us yearn to pick them up and put them in our pockets as a keepsake and to rub their smooth, cool surfaces.

This is the sophisticated beach-front house in southern California built in 1995 to the designs of architect Rob Quigley. The interior walls are bare concrete, their velvety surface providing inspiration for a soft grey painted finish.

Bleached branches of wood lie against a mud wall in the Yemen, creating a composition in desert shades.

This fabulous fusion of northern and southern styles – European upholstery, Moorish furniture and details – is decorated in creams and browns with brightening touches of saffron, fuscia and flame.

The home-made ceremonial masks of Mudmen in Papua New Guinea, and the colour of the men's bodies, are at one with the landscape, being the same shade of grey as the local soil.

KALEIDOSCOPE

The rich and appealing patterns on an ancient flint-laid wall reveal the skill and imagination of nameless craftsmen and builders in centuries past.

The natural world inspires us with sometimes astonishing colour combinations. Here, the egg-yolk yellow sings with the blue-black and white of a shoal of Pacific double-saddle butterfly fish, seen near Bora Bora.

Frank O. Gehry designed the stunning titanium-plated Guggenheim Museum in Bilbao, Spain. Its gleaming silver skin and futuristic form are a link with this city's fine but faded industrial heritage.

Juicy, flavoured traditional jelly babies are jumbled in a glorious kaleidoscope of colour, in a sweet shop in Cheddar Gorge, England.

Owners Jason McCoy and Diana Burroughs found this federal house in Cooperstown, New York State, almost untouched from the time it was built in 1815. Jaques Dehornois helped them decorate the interior sparingly, with authentic colonial colours. The 'sculpture' is a Victorian hat rack.

Reels of thread organized by colour make the one you want easier to find, and at the same time are a visual delight.

Once a garage, now a studio and summer bedroom, this rough-hewn timber structure has been coloured a steely rugged grey with matt painting, bringing it into tune with the massive stainless steel sink installed for garden chores.

Gloriously coloured and patterned spinnaker sails billow out as sailors vie to extract every ounce of power from the wind, in this race in the sunshine off Key West, Florida.

Artist Kate Blee appreciates the visual interest created by staircase and doors, pillars and balusters, and has kept the colours simple – white paint, muted grey paint and shades of brown – for a calming effect.

Four colours – shades of the primaries red, blue and yellow, with green – have been applied to timber beach huts along a seafront in South Africa to create a festive vista.

Sacks of spices, their roasted colours a draw to the eye, are waiting for customers in a market in the Yemen.

An equally zany interior to Mary Rose Young's, this bedroom will keep you awake till the lights go out with its painted decorations – orange and red striped walls and animal 'print' ceiling, skirting and window frame.

Reds and greens, yellows and purples – two pairs of complementary colours mingle in these crates of mangoes fresh from the market.

The bright tunnel-vision effect created by French artist Robert Delaunay, in his painting entitled *Political Drama* (1914) draws the viewer in through its vibrant colour and sense of spiralling movement.

Of all the blue pigments available to make paint, none is more beguiling than ultramarine blue which tends towards purple, and pale blues made with this pigment have a warm Mediterranean feel. The image shows 'Solent Blue Distemper' from Fired Earth's English Palette, by Kevin McCloud.

A work of art in itself, a Rajput Maharaja's eye-catching and elaborate headdress, on parade in Jodhpur in the State of Rajasthan, India.

This strikingly rich violet tone is typical of the richer spectrum of colours used in Mackintosh interiors. The image shows a wash of the colour 'Thistle' from the Art Nouveau range of colours, produced by Fired Earth in conjunction with the Victoria & Albert Museum in London.

The decoration of this room is composed of solid blocks of different bright colours, which provide a dramatic backdrop to other vibrantly bright-coloured objects and furnishings and to the naïve energy of handmade animal masks.

A door in a white wall opens to reveal brilliant colour within, while pillars in this loft home by Architect Will White in Shoredich, London, are clad in purple. Bright colour is invigorating rather than overwhelming if you use it with plenty of white, neutrals or pale tones.

The home of designer Ozwald Boateng is an advertisement for his bold, contemporary use of colour and pattern in a traditional setting.

Red, blue, purple, yellow, orange, green... by using these carefully toned colours with plenty of cream and white, Pentagram designers in New York have created a rich but not exhausting interior. The textured rug by Christine Vanderhurd invites touch.

Designer Mary Rose Young is known for her flamboyant decorated pottery – now she has applied way-out pattern to the surfaces of walls and furniture in her cottage in the Forest of Dean, England.

INDEX

THANK YOU

Elizabeth Hilliard and Stafford Cliff are terrifically grateful to the following people and organizations for their generous assistance:

Mr and Mrs Richard Anderson
Zoe Antoniou at Pavilion Books
Mandy Aspinall
Nadine Bazar
Antony Beevor
Felicity Bryan and her team, especially
    Michele Topham
Judy Cox
Craig & Rose plc
Mr and Mrs David Hilliard
Mr and Mrs Andrew Jolliffe
Hardy Jones
New Guard Decorator Centre, Wakefield
Una Richards and The Traditional Paint
    Forum
The Johnstone Group Ltd
John Scott
William Selka
Kulbir Thandi
Andrew Townsend

PICTURE CREDITS

BACK COVER
© VT Wonen/Dennis Brandsma.

INTRODUCTION
6 Paul Ryan/International Interiors; 7 The Interior Archive/Wayne Vincent; 10 Kulbir Thandi; 12 Marie Claire Maison/Nicolas Tosi/Catherine Ardouin; 13 Kulbir Thandi; 16–17 © Stephen White/Small Circles Painting by Peter Davies courtesy of the Saatchi Gallery, London; 24–25 Gettyone Stone/Mike Magnuson.

ARCTIC TINTS
28 ffotograff/Patricia Aithie; 29 Frank Lane Picture Library/E & D Hosking; 30 ffotograff/Patricia Aithie; 31 Gettyone Stone/Ernst Haas; 32 Gettyone Stone/Daniel J Cox; 33 Christian Sarramon; 34 Axiom/Chris Parker; 35 John Miller; 36 Narratives/Jan Baldwin/Lena Proudlock – Denim in Style tel: 01666 890230; 37 Paul Ryan/International Interiors; 38–39 Axiom/James Morris.

OCEAN WASH
54 Brian & Cherry Alexander; 55 Impact Photos/Yann Arthus Bertrand/with Fuji Film; 56 Colorsport; 57 Frank Lane Picture Library/Martin Withers; 58 S & O Mathews; 59 Hémisphères/Patrick Frilet; 60 Frank Lane Picture Library/Chris Mattison; 61 Marcus Harpur; 62 Christian Sarramon; 63 Deidi von Schaewen; 64 Robert O'Dea; 65 Christian Sarramon; 66 Narratives/Jan Baldwin/Lena Proudlock – Denim in Style tel: 01666 890230; 67 www.elizabethwhiting.com/Spike Powell; 68 Red Cover/Jake Fitzjones; 69 Ricardo Labougle; 70 Marie Claire Maison/Gilles de Chabaneix; 71 Jonty Henshall tel: 07811 414364.

FOREST HUES
80 S & O Mathews; 81 Jerry Harpur; 82 Gettyone Stone/Art Wolfe; 83 Gettyone Stone/Jerry Alexander; 84 Impact Photos/Catriona Bass; 85 ffotograff/Patricia Aithie; 86 World of Interiors/Timothy Soar; 87 Christian Sarramon; 88 World of Interiors/James Mortimer; 89 New York Style by Suzanne Slesin, Daniel Rozensztroch & Stafford Cliff. Photographs by Gilles de Chabaneix; 90–91 David Seidner; 92 VT Wonen/Dennis Brandsma; 93 Marie Claire Maison/Marie Pierre Morel/Christine Puech.

EARTH TONES
104 Mark Bolton; 105 NHPA/Daniel Zupanc; 106 Frank Lane Picture Library/J McDonald/Sunset; 107 Gettyone Stone/Terry Vine; 108 Kulbir Thandi; 109 Gettyone Stone/Thomas Brase; 110 Tim Winters; 111 Tessa Traeger; 112 Alexander van Berge; 113 Marie Claire Maison/Gilles de Chabaneix/Catherine Ardouin; 114 Christian Sarramon; 115 Paul Ryan/International Interiors; 118 Marie Claire Maison/Marie Pierre Morel/Gerald le Signe; 119 Narratives/Jan Baldwin/Tatyana Hill – Immaculate House tel: 020 7499 5758.

DESERT SHADES
130 Gettyone Stone/Ed Collacott; 131 Bridgeman Art Library/Scottish National Gallery of Modern Art, Edinburgh/artist Giorgio Morandi/© DACS 2001; 132 Gettyone Stone/Paul Kenward; 133 Frank Lane Picture Library/Terry Whittaker; 134 Gettyone Stone/World Perspectives; 135 Gettyone Stone/Darrell Gulin; 136 Axiom/Luke White; 137 Gettyone Stone/Christopher Arnesen; 138 Deidi von Schaewen; 139 Travel Ink/Chris Stammers; 140–141 New York Style by Suzanne Slesin, Daniel Rozensztroch & Stafford Cliff. Photographs by Gilles de Chabaneix; 142 The Interior Archive/Andrew Wood; 143 IPC International Syndication/© Homes & Gardens/Caroline Arber; 144 Undine Pröhl; 145 VT Wonen/Dennis Brandsma.

KALEIDOSCOPE
154–155 Gettyone Stone/Art Wolfe; 158 ffotograff/Patricia Aithie; 159 Jacqui Hurst; 160 Kos Picture Source/Kos; 161 Deidi von Schaewen; 162 Axiom/Luke White; 163 Gettyone Stone/Kristin Finnegan; 164 National Gallery of Washington/Political Drama, artist Robert Delaunay. Gift of the Joseph H Hazen Foundation, Inc., © 2000 Board of Trustees, National Gallery of Art, Washington, 1914, oil and collage on cardboard; 165 Paul Harris; 166 Marie Claire Maison/Gilles de Chabaneix/Caroline Tiné/Daniel Rozensztroch; 167 Christoph Kicherer; 168 The Interior Archive/Tim Clinch; 169 Houses & Interiors/Verne; 170 www.elizabethwhiting.com/Andreas von Einseidel; 171 The Interior Archive/Edina van der Wyck/designer Shari Maryon.

IDEAS IN PRACTICE
Blue bedroom by Tim Mercer.